2008
Children Welcome!
Family Holiday & Days Out Guide

Family-Friendly Pubs,
Britain's Blue Flag and Award-Winning Beaches

2

Maps: ©MAPS IN MINUTES™ / Collins Bartholomew 2007

Typeset by FHG Guides Ltd, Paisley.
Printed and bound in Malaysia by Imago.

Distribution. Book Trade: ORCA Book Services, Stanley House,
3 Fleets Lane, Poole, Dorset BH15 3AJ
(Tel: 01202 665432; Fax: 01202 666219)
e-mail: mail@orcabookservices.co.uk
Published by FHG Guides Ltd., Abbey Mill Business Centre,
Seedhill, Paisley PA1 ITJ (Tel: 0141-887 0428; Fax: 0141-889 7204).
e-mail: admin@fhguides.co.uk

Children Welcome! Family Holidays & Days Out Guide is published by FHG Guides Ltd,
part of Kuperard Group.

Cover design: FHG Guides
Cover Pictures: Langstone Cliff Hotel, South Devon (see advertisement on inside back cover).

Acknowledgements

Our thanks for pictures courtesy of:

Kent Tourism (p45), Woodlands Leisure Park (p67)
Devon County Council (p74, 75), Poole Tourism (p90),
Eastbourne Borough Council (p102), Whitby Borough Council (p131),
Blackpool Borough Council Tourism (p135),
Galloway Wildlife Conservation Park (p145),

Contents

LEGOLAND® WINDSOR SCORES A 'MOLE-IN-ONE'

A new 18-hole mini-golf attraction called 'Mole-In-One' has opened at LEGOLAND® Windsor. The woodland-themed course includes LEGO® brick models of squirrels, foxes, moles and otters as well as beautiful water features set in a stunning landscaped location.

Each hole has a different woodland animal theme and like all of the park's attractions, they focus on interactive, hands-on entertainment. There is even a special 'Heroes Hole' just for younger golfers so playing against an adult couldn't be more fun!

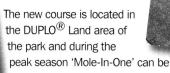

The new course is located in the DUPLO® Land area of the park and during the peak season 'Mole-In-One' can be separated into two nine hole courses to reduce waiting times. One of the nine hole courses is fully wheelchair accessible.

National leisure contractor, Western Log Group, was commissioned to build the £300,000 outdoor attraction and this latest addition to the Berkshire theme park is a joint venture project between two companies.

Vicky Brown, general manager of LEGOLAND® Windsor commented: "Our attractions are all about interacting and learning through play. The Mole-In-One mini-golf course allows children to practice new skills and have fun with their families at the same time so fits perfectly into a day here at the park."

LEGOLAND. WINDSOR®

www.legoland.co.uk

How To Use This Guide

The guide offers information on good beaches, resorts and visits, plus comprehensive coverage of Family Holiday Accommodation.

The order is geographical, starting with Cornwall and working eastwards through Devon, Somerset, Dorset and around the South Coast to London before moving northwards to Scotland, and then to Wales.

For 2008 we have once again included our Vouchers with FREE and REDUCED RATE entry to holiday attractions throughout the country. See pages 9-44.

Detailed page references are provided on contents page 3.

Starting from page 165 are the summarised accommodation listings, classified in the same county order as the main guide and with detailed information in symbol form. This easy reference guide will help you to make preliminary selections, if you wish, of the kind of accommodation and facilities which you feel are most suitable.

On pages 177-180 we once again include the supplement, "Family Friendly Pubs, Inns and Hotels", a brief list of some establishments which have indicated that they particularly welcome children. Please note that not all the hotels/inns featured here have advertisements in this Guide.

A useful index of towns and the sections in which they appear is featured on page 181

Up to £25 off entrance to LEGOLAND® Windsor*

Excluding August *£5 off for up to 5 people

Vikings are invading LEGOLAND Windsor!

Check out the amazing, humungous and hilarious Vikings' River Splash ride. Take a wild, wet voyage through a Viking world built from thousands of LEGO® bricks but try to avoid a complete soaking.

Complete family travel protection. It's right in front of your nose!

Travel insurance for 2 weeks in Spain for a family costs under £30[†] plus children go free

Why Choose  FACTOR 50 Travel Insurance from Barnardo's

- Children go for free with family cover
- Single trip or annual policies to suit your holiday needs
- Great value for money
- Available to UK residents up to age 74 years
- 10% online discount when you buy at www.barnardos.org.uk/factor50
- Annual policies which allow you to go on an unlimited number of leisure trips (maximum 31 days per trip)
- Winter sports cover option
- 24 hour emergency medical helpline

● Buy online – and save 10%

You can buy Factor 50 cover immediately at www.barnardos.org.uk/factor50 (quoting promo code CW08) What's more, if you buy online, you'll benefit from a 10% discount

● Call us for a quote and buy over the phone

Just call us on 0845 260 1587 (quoting promo code CW08) and one of our advisors will be happy to answer your questions. We are open between 8am-6pm Monday-Friday, except on Bank Holidays

Barnardo's
BELIEVE IN CHILDREN

FACTOR 50 Travel Insurance from Barnardo's

Great value travel insurance for you and your family

England and Wales • Counties

NORTHUMBERLAND

TYNE & WEAR

DURHAM
43

CUMBRIA
42 41 40 39

ISLE OF MAN

NORTH YORKSHIRE

38 EAST RIDING OF YORKSHIRE

LANCASHIRE
34
WEST YORKSHIRE
37
33
36 35
GREATER
MANCHESTER S. YORKSHIRE
32
30
31

ISLE OF ANGLESEY

CONWY b CHESHIRE DERBYSHIRE LINCOLNSHIRE
a NOTTINGHAMSHIRE
c 29
GWYNEDD 27 26
STAFFORDSHIRE
28 LEICESTERSHIRE RUTLAND
25 24 NORFOLK

SHROPSHIRE WEST
MIDLANDS

CEREDIGION POWYS WORCESTERSHIRE NORTHAMPTONSHIRE CAMBRIDGESHIRE SUFFOLK
WARWICKSHIRE
HEREFORDSHIRE
23 BEDFORDSHIRE
CARMARTHENSHIRE 22
PEMBROKESHIRE BUCKINGHAMSHIRE ESSEX
GLOUCESTERSHIRE HERTFORDSHIRE
d e h l m o OXFORDSHIRE
g k 12 10
f n 17 16 15 11 GREATER 9
i j 21 14 13 LONDON 8
20 19 18 SURREY KENT
WILTSHIRE

SOMERSET HAMPSHIRE

DEVON WEST SUSSEX EAST SUSSEX
DORSET 3 4 5 6 7
CORNWALL ISLE OF WIGHT
1 2

Unitary Authorities – England & Wales

1. Plymouth
2. Torbay
3. Poole
4. Bournemouth
5. Southampton
6. Portsmouth
7. Brighton & Hove
8. Medway
9. Thurrock
10. Southend
11. Slough
12. Windsor & Maidenhead
13. Bracknell Forest
14. Wokingham
15. Reading
16. West Berkshire
17. Swindon
18. Bath & Northeast Somerset
19. North Somerset
20. Bristol
21. South Gloucestershire
22. Luton
23. Milton Keynes
24. Peterborough
25. Leicester
26. Nottingham
27. Derby
28. Telford & Wrekin
29. Stoke-on-Trent
30. Warrington
31. Halton
32. Merseyside
33. Blackburn with Darwen
34. Blackpool
35. N.E. Lincolnshire
36. North Lincolnshire
37. Kingston-upon-Hull
38. York
39. Redcar & Cleveland
40. Middlesborough
41. Stockton-on-Tees
42. Darlington
43. Hartlepool

NORTH WALES
a. Denbighshire
b. Flintshire
c. Wrexham

SOUTH WALES
d. Swansea
e. Neath & Port Talbot
f. Bridgend
g. Rhondda Cynon Taff
h. Merthyr Tydfil
i. Vale of Glamorgan
j. Cardiff
k. Caerphilly
l. Blaenau Gwent
m. Torfaen
n. Newport
o. Monmouthshire

9

LEIGHTON BUZZARD RAILWAY

Page's Park Station, Billington Road,
Leighton Buzzard, Bedfordshire LU7 4TN
Tel: 01525 373888
e-mail: info@buzzrail.co.uk
www.buzzrail.co.uk

READERS' OFFER 2008

One FREE adult/child with full-fare adult ticket
Valid 11/3/2008 - 28/10/2008

NOT TO BE USED IN CONJUNCTION WITH ANY OTHER OFFER

THE LIVING RAINFOREST

Hampstead Norreys,
Berkshire RG18 0TN
Tel: 01635 202444 • Fax: 01635 202440
e-mail: enquiries@livingrainforest.org
www.livingrainforest.org

READERS' OFFER 2008

One FREE child with each full paying adult.
Valid during 2008.

NOT TO BE USED IN CONJUNCTION WITH ANY OTHER OFFER

BEKONSCOT MODEL VILLAGE & RAILWAY

Warwick Road, Beaconsfield,
Buckinghamshire HP9 2PL
Tel: 01494 672919
e-mail: info@bekonscot.co.uk
www.bekonscot.com

READERS' OFFER 2008

One child FREE when accompanied by full-paying adult
Valid February to October 2008

NOT TO BE USED IN CONJUNCTION WITH ANY OTHER OFFER

BUCKINGHAMSHIRE RAILWAY CENTRE

Quainton Road Station, Quainton,
Aylesbury HP22 4BY
Tel & Fax: 01296 655720
e-mail: bucksrailcentre@btopenworld.com
www.bucksrailcentre.org

READERS' OFFER 2008

One child FREE with each full-paying adult
Not valid for Special Events

NOT TO BE USED IN CONJUNCTION WITH ANY OTHER OFFER

A 70-minute journey into the lost world of the English narrow gauge light railway. Features historic steam locomotives from many countries.

PETS MUST BE KEPT UNDER CONTROL AND NOT ALLOWED ON TRACKS

Open: Sundays and Bank Holiday weekends 11 March to 28 October. Additional days in summer.

Directions: on A4146 towards Hemel Hempstead, close to roundabout junction with A505.

Discover the exotic collection of tropical plants and animals inhabiting this living re-creation of the rainforest under glass. Explore your impact on the world's ecosystems using interactive displays. All-weather attraction. Children's play area.

Open: daily 10am to 5.15pm. Closed over Christmas period.

Directions: clearly signposted from J13 of M4. From Oxford take A34, exit at East Ilsley and follow signs. Nearest mainline station Newbury (8 miles). £1 'green discount' for visitors arriving by bus or bike.

Be a giant in a magical miniature world of make-believe depicting rural England in the 1930s. "A little piece of history that is forever England."

Open: 10am-5pm daily mid February to end October.

Directions: Junction 16 M25, Junction 2 M40.

A working steam railway centre. Steam train rides, miniature railway rides, large collection of historic preserved steam locomotives, carriages and wagons.

Open: Sundays and Bank Holidays April to October, plus Wednesdays in school holidays 10.30am to 4.30pm.

Directions: off A41 Aylesbury to Bicester Road, 6 miles north west of Aylesbury.

12

Birds of Prey Centre offering
audience participation in flying
displays which are held 3 times daily.
Tours, picnic area, gift shop,
tearoom, craft shop.

Open: 10am-5pm all year except
Christmas and New Year.

Directions: follow brown tourist
signs from B1040.

FHG GUIDES, ABBEY MILL BUSINESS CENTRE, PAISLEY PA1 1TJ • www.holidayguides.com

Farm animals, Shire Horse Centre,
18th century watermill and
farmhouse, farm artifacts, caravan
and camping,
children's play areas.
Cafe and farm & gift shop.

Open: all year.
9.30am to 5pm 1st March -30th Sept
10am-4pm 1st Oct to 28th Feb

Directions: signposted off both
A47 and A1.

FHG GUIDES, ABBEY MILL BUSINESS CENTRE, PAISLEY PA1 1TJ • www.holidayguides.com

Can you imagine your family living in
a space measuring 6' x 8'?
Clamber aboard our collection of
narrowboats. New interactive
galleries, shop, cafe. Large free car
park. Daily boat trips.

Open: 10am to 5pm daily

Directions: Junction 9 off the M53,
signposted.

FHG GUIDES, ABBEY MILL BUSINESS CENTRE, PAISLEY PA1 1TJ • www.holidayguides.com

The Country Park covers 26 acres
and includes woodland and historic
trails, picnic sites, children's
adventure trail and award-winning
cycle trail. Remains of a Victorian
clay works complete with the largest
working water wheel in Cornwall.
Shop, cafe, exhibitions, museum.

Open: 10am-6pm daily (closed
Christmas Day)

Directions: two miles north of
St Austell on the B3274. Follow
brown tourist signs. 5 minutes from
Eden Project.

FHG GUIDES, ABBEY MILL BUSINESS CENTRE, PAISLEY PA1 1TJ • www.holidayguides.com

13

GEEVOR TIN MINE
Pendeen, Penzance,
Cornwall TR19 7EW
Tel: 01736 788662 • Fax: 01736 786059
e-mail: bookings@geevor.com
www.geevor.com

READERS' OFFER 2008

TWO for the price of ONE or £3.75 off a family ticket
Valid 02/01/2008 to 20/12/2008

NOT TO BE USED IN CONJUNCTION WITH ANY OTHER OFFER

NATIONAL SEAL SANCTUARY
Gweek, Helston,
Cornwall TR12 6UG
Tel: 01326 221361
e-mail: seals@sealsanctuary.co.uk
www.sealsanctuary.co.uk

READERS' OFFER 2008

TWO for ONE - on purchase of another ticket of
equal or greater value. Valid until December 2008.

NOT TO BE USED IN CONJUNCTION WITH ANY OTHER OFFER

TAMAR VALLEY DONKEY PARK
St Ann's Chapel, Gunnislake,
Cornwall PL18 9HW
Tel: 01822 834072
e-mail: info@donkeypark.com
www.donkeypark.com

READERS' OFFER 2008

50p OFF per person, up to 6 persons
Valid from Easter until end October 2008

NOT TO BE USED IN CONJUNCTION WITH ANY OTHER OFFER

DUCKY'S PARK FARM
Moor Lane, Flookburgh, Grange-over-Sands
Cumbria LA11 7LS
Tel: 015395 59293 • Fax: 015395 58005
e-mail: donna@duckysparkfarm.co.uk
www.duckysparkfarm.co.uk

READERS' OFFER 2008

10% OFF admission price
Valid during 2008

NOT TO BE USED IN CONJUNCTION WITH ANY OTHER OFFER

14

Geevor is the largest mining history site in the UK in a spectacular setting on Cornwall's Atlantic coast. Guided underground tour, many surface buildings, museum, cafe, gift shop. Free parking.

Open: daily except Saturdays 10am to 4pm

Directions: 7 miles from Penzance beside the B3306 Land's End to St Ives coast road

Britain's leading grey seal rescue centre

Open: daily (except Christmas Day) from 10am

Directions: from A30 follow signs to Helston, then brown tourist signs to Seal Sanctuary.

Cornwall's only Donkey Sanctuary set in 14 acres overlooking the beautiful Tamar Valley. Donkey rides, rabbit warren, goat hill, children's playgrounds, cafe and picnic area. New all-weather play barn.

Open: Easter to end Oct: daily 10am to 5.30pm. Nov to March: weekends and all school holidays 10.30am to 4.30pm

Directions: just off A390 between Callington and Gunnislake at St Ann's Chapel.

Children's open farm animal interaction centre. Large indoor soft play, bouncy castle, go-karts, driving school, playground, cafe. Full disabled facilities, wheelchair-friendly.

Open: March to October 10.30am to 4pm

Directions: M6 J36. Follow A590 through Grange-over-Sands on the B5277. From Barrow-in-Furness turn right at Haverthwaite on to the B278 and follow signs to Flookburgh.

CARS OF THE STARS MOTOR MUSEUM
Standish Street, Keswick,
Cumbria CA12 5HH
Tel: 017687 73757
e-mail: cotsmm@aol.com
www.carsofthestars.com

READERS' OFFER 2008

One child free with two paying adults
Valid during 2008

NOT TO BE USED IN CONJUNCTION WITH ANY OTHER OFFER

ESKDALE HISTORIC WATER MILL
Mill Cottage, Boot, Eskdale,
Cumbria CA19 1TG
Tel: 019467 23335
e-mail: david.king403@tesco.net
www.eskdale.info

Eskdale
Historic
Water Mill

READERS' OFFER 2008

Two children FREE with two adults
Valid during 2008

NOT TO BE USED IN CONJUNCTION WITH ANY OTHER OFFER

CRICH TRAMWAY VILLAGE
Crich, Matlock
Derbyshire DE4 5DP
Tel: 01773 854321 • Fax: 01773 854320
e-mail: enquiry@tramway.co.uk
www.tramway.co.uk

READERS' OFFER 2008

One child FREE with every full-paying adult
Valid during 2008

NOT TO BE USED IN CONJUNCTION WITH ANY OTHER OFFER

DEVONSHIRE COLLECTION OF PERIOD COSTUME
Totnes Costume Museum,
Bogan House, 43 High Street,
Totnes,
Devon TQ9 5NP

READERS' OFFER 2008

FREE child with a paying adult with voucher
Valid from Spring Bank Holiday to end of Sept 2008

NOT TO BE USED IN CONJUNCTION WITH ANY OTHER OFFER

A collection of cars from film and TV, including Chitty Chitty Bang Bang, James Bond's Aston Martin, Del Boy's van, Fab1 and many more.

PETS MUST BE KEPT ON LEAD

Open: daily 10am-5pm. Open February half term, Ist April to end November, also weekends in December.

Directions: in centre of Keswick close to car park.

The oldest working mill in England with 18th century oatmeal machinery running daily.

DOGS ON LEADS

Open: 11am to 5pm April to Sept. (may be closed Saturdays & Mondays)

Directions: near inland terminus of Ravenglass & Eskdale Railway or over Hardknott Pass.

A superb family day out in the atmosphere of a bygone era. Explore the recreated period street and fascinating exhibitions. Unlimited tram rides are free with entry. Play areas, woodland walk and sculpture trail, shops, tea rooms, pub, restaurant and lots more.

Open: daily April to October 10 am to 5.30pm, weekends in winter.

Directions: eight miles from M1 Junction 28, follow brown and white signs for "Tramway Museum".

Themed exhibition, changed annually, based in a Tudor house. Collection contains items of dress for women, men and children from 17th century to 1980s, from high fashion to everyday wear.

Open: Open from Spring Bank Holiday to end September. 11am to 5pm Tuesday to Friday.

Directions: centre of town, opposite Market Square. Mini bus up High Street stops outside.

WOODLANDS
Blackawton, Dartmouth,
Devon TQ9 7DQ
Tel: 01803 712598 • Fax: 01803 712680
e-mail: fun@woodlandspark.com
www.woodlandspark.com

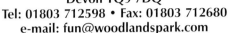

READERS' OFFER 2008

12% discount off individual entry price for up to 4 persons. No photocopies. Valid 15/3/08 – 1/11/08

NOT TO BE USED IN CONJUNCTION WITH ANY OTHER OFFER

KILLHOPE LEAD MINING MUSEUM
Cowshill, Upper Weardale,
Co. Durham DL13 1AR
Tel: 01388 537505
e-mail: killhope@durham.gov.uk
www.durham.gov.uk/killhope

READERS' OFFER 2008

*One child FREE with full-paying adult
Valid April to October 2008*

NOT TO BE USED IN CONJUNCTION WITH ANY OTHER OFFER

TWEDDLE CHILDREN'S ANIMAL FARM
Fillpoke Lane, Blackhall Colliery,
Co. Durham TS27 4BT
Tel: 0191 586 3311
e-mail: info@tweddle-farm.co.uk
www.tweddle-farm.co.uk

READERS' OFFER 2008

*FREE bag of animal food to every paying customer.
Valid until end 2008*

NOT TO BE USED IN CONJUNCTION WITH ANY OTHER OFFER

ST AUGUSTINE'S FARM
Arlingham
Gloucestershire GL2 7JN
Tel & Fax: 01452 740277
staugustines@btconnect.com
www.staugustinesfarm.co.uk

READERS' OFFER 2008

*One child FREE with paying adult.
Valid March to October 2008.*

NOT TO BE USED IN CONJUNCTION WITH ANY OTHER OFFER

All weather fun - guaranteed! Unique combination of indoor/outdoor attractions. 3 Watercoasters, Toboggan Run, Arctic Gliders, boats, 15 Playzones for all ages. Biggest indoor venture zone in UK with 5 floors of play and rides. New Big Fun Farm with U-drive Tractor ride, Pedal Town and Yard Racers. Falconry Centre.

Open: mid-March to November open daily at 9.30am. Winter: open weekends and local school holidays.

Directions: 5 miles from Dartmouth on A3122. Follow brown tourist signs from A38.

This award-winning Victorian mining museum makes a great day out for all the family. Hands-on activities plus unforgettable mine tour. Green Tourism Gold Award 2007.

Open: Easter weekend +April 1st to October 31st 10.30am to 5pm daily.

Directions: alongside A689, midway between Stanhope and Alston in the heart of the North Pennines.

Children's farm and petting centre with lots of farm animals and exotic animals too, including camels, otters, monkeys, meerkats and lots more. Lots of hands-on, with bottle feeding, reptile handling and bunny cuddling happening daily.

Open: March to Oct: 10am-5pm daily; Nov to Feb 10am to 4pm daily. Closed Christmas, Boxing Day and New Year's Day.

Directions: A181 from A19, head towards coast; signposted from there.

A real working organic dairy farm in the Severn Vale. St Augustine's is a typical dairy farm of over 100 acres where the everyday farm life will go on around you.

Open: March to October open daily 11am to 5pm (except term-time Mondays).

Directions: leave M5 by J13 to A38. Half a mile south turn right on B4071 and follow brown tourist signs.

AVON VALLEY RAILWAY
Bitton Station, Bath Road, Bitton,
Bristol BS30 6HD
Tel: 0117 932 5538
e-mail: info@avonvalleyrailway.org
www.avonvalleyrailway.org

READERS' OFFER 2008

One FREE child with every fare-paying adult
Valid May - Oct 2008 (not 'Day Out with Thomas' events)

NOT TO BE USED IN CONJUNCTION WITH ANY OTHER OFFER

EXPLOSION! MUSEUM OF NAVAL FIREPOWER
Priddy's Hard, Gosport
Hampshire PO12 4LE
Tel: 023 9250 5600 • Fax: 023 9250 5605
e-mail: info@explosion.org.uk
www.explosion.org.uk

READERS' OFFER 2008

SPECIAL OFFER 2008 - entry for just £1 per person.
One person per voucher. Not valid for events tickets.

NOT TO BE USED IN CONJUNCTION WITH ANY OTHER OFFER

QUEX MUSEUM, HOUSE & GARDENS
Quex Park, Birchington
Kent CT7 0BH
Tel: 01843 842168 • Fax: 01843 846661
e-mail: enquiries@quexmuseum.org
www.quexmuseum.org

READERS' OFFER 2008

One adult FREE with each full-paying adult on
presentation of voucher. Valid until 31 December 2008

NOT TO BE USED IN CONJUNCTION WITH ANY OTHER OFFER

CHISLEHURST CAVES
Old Hill, Chislehurst,
Kent BR7 5NB
Tel: 020 8467 3264 • Fax: 020 8295 0407
e-mail: info@chislehurstcaves.co.uk
www.chislehurstcaves.co.uk

READERS' OFFER 2008

FREE child entry with full paying adult.
Valid until end 2008 (not Bank Holiday weekends)

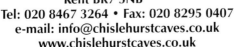

NOT TO BE USED IN CONJUNCTION WITH ANY OTHER OFFER

The Avon Valley Railway offers a whole new experience for some, and a nostalgic memory for others.

PETS MUST BE KEPT ON LEADS AND OFF TRAIN SEATS

Open: Steam trains operate every Sunday, Easter to October, plus Bank Holidays and Christmas.

Directions: on the A431 midway between Bristol and Bath at Bitton.

A hands-on interactive museum, telling the story of naval warfare from gunpowder to modern missiles. Also fascinating social history of how 2500 women worked on the site during World War II. Gift shop and Waterside Coffee Shop with stunning harbour views.

Open: Saturday and Sunday 10am to 4pm (last entry one hour before closing).

Directions: M27 to J11, follow A32 to Gosport; signposted. By rail to Portsmouth Harbour, then ferry to Gosport.

World-ranking Museum incorporating Kent's finest Regency house. Gardens with peacocks, woodland walk, walled garden, maze and fountains. Children's activities and full events programme. Tearoom and gift shop.

Open: mid-March-Nov: Sun-Thurs 11am-5pm (House opens 2pm). Winter: Sundays 1-3.30pm (Museum and Gardens only).

Directions: A2 to Margate, on entering Birchington turn right at church into Park Lane; Quex Museum signposted.

Miles of mystery and history beneath your feet! Grab a lantern and get ready for an amazing underground adventure. Your whole family can travel back in time as you explore this labyrinth of dark mysterious passageways. See the caves, church, Druid altar and more.

Open: Wed to Sun from 10am; last tour 4pm. Open daily during local school and Bank holidays (except Christmas). Entrance by guided tour only.

Directions: A222 between A20 and A21; at Chislehurst Station turn into Station Approach; turn right at end, then right again into Caveside Close.

WINGHAM WILDLIFE PARK

Rusham Road, Wingham,
Canterbury, Kent CT3 1JL
Tel: 01227 720836
gabr@winghamwildlifepark.co.uk
www.winghamwildlifepark.co.uk

K·U·P·E·R·A·R·D

**READERS'
OFFER
2008**

One FREE child entry with two full paying adults

NOT TO BE USED IN CONJUNCTION WITH ANY OTHER OFFER

THE HOP FARM AT THE KENTISH OAST VILLAGE

Beltring, Paddock Wood,
Kent TN12 6PY
Tel: 01622 872068 • Fax: 01622 870800
e-mail: info@thehopfarm.co.uk
www.thehopfarm.co.uk

K·U·P·E·R·A·R·D

**READERS'
OFFER
2008**

*Admit one child HALF PRICE with a full paying adult.
Valid until March 2008.*

NOT TO BE USED IN CONJUNCTION WITH ANY OTHER OFFER

MUSEUM OF KENT LIFE

Lock Lane, Sandling, Maidstone,
Kent ME14 3AU
Tel: 01622 763936 • Fax: 01622 662024
e-mail: enquiries@museum-kentlife.co.uk
www.museum-kentlife.co.uk

MUSEUM OF
KENT LIFE

K·U·P·E·R·A·R·D

**READERS'
OFFER
2008**

*One child FREE with one full-paying adult
Valid during 2008*

NOT TO BE USED IN CONJUNCTION WITH ANY OTHER OFFER

DOCKER PARK FARM

Arkholme, Carnforth,
Lancashire LA6 1AR
Tel & Fax: 015242 21331
e-mail: info@dockerparkfarm.co.uk
www.dockerparkfarm.co.uk

K·U·P·E·R·A·R·D

**READERS'
OFFER
2008**

*One FREE child per one paying adult (one voucher per child)
Valid from January to December 2008*

NOT TO BE USED IN CONJUNCTION WITH ANY OTHER OFFER

Come and join us .. .take a walk on the wildside ... see meerkats, lemurs, reptile house, birds of prey, pet village, parrot house and much more. With an adventure playground and full facilities, you'll be sure to enjoy your day.

Open: daily 10am to 6pm or dusk (whichever is earlier). Guide dogs only.

Directions: on the A257 main Sandwich to Canterbury road, just outside the village.

FHG GUIDES, ABBEY MILL BUSINESS CENTRE, PAISLEY PA1 1TJ • www.holidayguides.com

Set in 400 acres of unspoilt Kent countryside, this once working hop farm is one of Kent's most popular attractions. The spectacular oast village is home to an indoor and outdoor play area, interactive museum, shire horses and an animal farm, as well as hosting special events throughout the year.

Open: 10am-5pm daily (last admission 4pm).

Directions: A228 Paddock Wood

FHG GUIDES, ABBEY MILL BUSINESS CENTRE, PAISLEY PA1 1TJ • www.holidayguides.com

Kent's award-winning open air museum is home to a collection of historic buildings which house interactive exhibitions on life over the last 150 years.

Open: seven days a week from February to start November, 10am to 5pm.

Directions: Junction 6 off M20, follow signs to Aylesford.

FHG GUIDES, ABBEY MILL BUSINESS CENTRE, PAISLEY PA1 1TJ • www.holidayguides.com

We are a working farm, with lots of animals to see and touch. Enjoy a walk round the Nature Trail or refreshments in the tearoom. Lots of activities during school holidays.

Open: Summer: daily 10.30am- 5pm. Winter: weekends only 10.30am-4pm.

Directions: Junction 35 off M6, take B6254 towards Kirkby Lonsdale, then follow the brown signs.

FHG GUIDES, ABBEY MILL BUSINESS CENTRE, PAISLEY PA1 1TJ • www.holidayguides.com

SKEGNESS NATURELAND SEAL SANCTUARY

North Parade, Skegness,
Lincolnshire PE25 1DB
Tel: 01754 764345
e-mail: natureland@fsbdial.co.uk
www.skegnessnatureland.co.uk

*Natureland
Seal Sanctuary*

READERS' OFFER 2008

Free entry for one child when accompanied by full-paying adult. Valid during 2008.

NOT TO BE USED IN CONJUNCTION WITH ANY OTHER OFFER

THE BEATLES STORY

Britannia Vaults, Albert Dock
Liverpool L3 4AD
Tel: 0151-709 1963 • Fax: 0151-708 0039
e-mail: info@beatlesstory.com
www.beatlesstory.com

READERS' OFFER 2008

*One FREE child with one full paying adult
Valid during 2008*

NOT TO BE USED IN CONJUNCTION WITH ANY OTHER OFFER

BRESSINGHAM STEAM & GARDENS

Low Road, Bressingham, Diss,
Norfolk IP22 2AB
Tel: 01379 686900 • Fax: 01379 686907
e-mail: info@bressingham.co.uk
www.bressingham.co.uk

READERS' OFFER 2008

*One child FREE with two paying adults
Valid Easter to October 2008*

NOT TO BE USED IN CONJUNCTION WITH ANY OTHER OFFER

FERRY FARM PARK

Ferry Farm, Boat Lane, Hoveringham
Nottinghamshire NG14 7JP
Tel & Fax: 0115 966 4512
e-mail: enquiries@ferryfarm.co.uk
www.ferryfarm.co.uk

READERS' OFFER 2008

*20% OFF admission price.
Valid during 2008.*

NOT TO BE USED IN CONJUNCTION WITH ANY OTHER OFFER

Well known for rescuing and rehabilitating orphaned and injured seal pups found washed ashore on Lincolnshire beaches. Also: penguins, aquarium, pets' corner, reptiles, Floral Palace (tropical birds and butterflies etc).

Open: daily from 10am. Closed Christmas/Boxing/New Year's Days.

Directions: at the north end of Skegness seafront.

FHG GUIDES, ABBEY MILL BUSINESS CENTRE, PAISLEY PA1 1TJ • www.holidayguides.com

---

A unique visitor attraction that transports you on an enlightening and atmospheric journey into the life, times, culture and music of the Beatles. See how four young lads from Liverpool were propelled into the dizzy heights of worldwide fame and fortune to become the greatest band of all time. Hear the story unfold through the 'Living History' audio guide narrated by John Lennon's sister, Julia.

Open: daily 10am to 6pm (last admisssion 5pm) all year round (excl. 25/26 December)

Directions: located within Liverpool's historic Albert Dock.

FHG GUIDES, ABBEY MILL BUSINESS CENTRE, PAISLEY PA1 1TJ • www.holidayguides.com

---

Explore one of Europe's leading steam collections, take a ride over 5 miles of narrow gauge steam railway, wander through beautiful gardens, or visit the only official 'Dads' Army' exhibition. Two restaurants and garden centre.

Open: Easter to October 10.30am - 5pm

Directions: 2½ miles west of Diss and 14 miles east of Thetford on the A1066; follow brown tourist signs.

FHG GUIDES, ABBEY MILL BUSINESS CENTRE, PAISLEY PA1 1TJ • www.holidayguides.com

---

Family-run farm park set in beautiful countryside next to river. 20-acre site with animal handling, large indoor soft play area, go-karts, trampolines, pedal tractors, swings, slides, zipline and assault course.

Open: daily 10am to 5.30pm April to end September. Closed Mondays except Bank Holidays and during school holidays. Please check for winter opening hours.

Directions: off A612 Nottingham to Southwell road.

FHG GUIDES, ABBEY MILL BUSINESS CENTRE, PAISLEY PA1 1TJ • www.holidayguides.com

NEWARK AIR MUSEUM
The Airfield, Winthorpe, Newark,
Nottinghamshire NG24 2NY
Tel: 01636 707170
e-mail: newarkair@onetel.com
www.newarkairmuseum.org

Party rate discount for every voucher (50p per person off normal admission). Valid during 2008.

NOT TO BE USED IN CONJUNCTION WITH ANY OTHER OFFER

THE TALES OF ROBIN HOOD
30 - 38 Maid Marian Way,
Nottingham NG1 6GF
Tel: 0115 9483284 • Fax: 0115 9501536
e-mail: robinhoodcentre@mail.com
www.robinhood.uk.com

*One FREE child with full paying adult per voucher
Valid from January to December 2008*

NOT TO BE USED IN CONJUNCTION WITH ANY OTHER OFFER

DIDCOT RAILWAY CENTRE
Didcot,
Oxfordshire OX11 7NJ
Tel: 01235 817200 • Fax: 01235 510621
e-mail: info@didcotrailwaycentre.org.uk
www.didcotrailwaycentre.org.uk

*One child FREE when accompanied by full-paying adult
Valid until end 2008 except during Day Out With Thomas events*

NOT TO BE USED IN CONJUNCTION WITH ANY OTHER OFFER

HOO FARM ANIMAL KINGDOM
Preston-on-the-Weald-Moors
Telford, Shropshire TF6 6DJ
Tel: 01952 677917 • Fax: 01952 677944
e-mail: info@hoofarm.com
www.hoofarm.com

*One child FREE with a full paying adult (one child per voucher).
Valid until Sept 2008 (not Bank Holiday Mondays). Closed Jan-March*

NOT TO BE USED IN CONJUNCTION WITH ANY OTHER OFFER

A collection of 70 aircraft and cockpit sections from across the history of aviation. Extensive aero engine and artefact displays.

Open: daily from 10am (closed Christmas period and New Year's Day).

Directions: follow brown and white signs from A1, A46, A17 and A1133.

Travel back in time with Robin Hood and his merry men on an adventure-packed theme tour, exploring the intriguing and mysterious story of their legendary tales of Medieval England. Enjoy film shows, live performances, adventure rides and even try archery! Are you brave enough to join Robin on his quest for good against evil?

Open: 10am-5.30pm, last admission 4.30pm.

Directions: follow the brown and white tourist information signs whilst heading towards the city centre.

See the steam trains from the golden age of the Great Western Railway. Steam locomotives in the original engine shed, a reconstructed country branch line, and a re-creation of Brunel's original broad gauge railway. On Steam Days there are rides in the 1930s carriages.

Open: Sat/Sun all year; daily 21 June to 31 August + school holidays. 10am-5pm weekends and Steam Days, 10am-4pm other days and in winter.

Directions: at Didcot Parkway rail station; on A4130, signposted from M4 (Junction 13) and A34

A real children's paradise. A complete hands-on experience, from feeding the lambs and sheep, goat racing, petting the lizards and talking to the parrots to candle dipping, mini quad biking, pony rides and other craft activities. Hoo Farm has everything for a family day out.

Open: follow brown tourist signs from M54 J6, A442 at Leegomery or A518 at Donnington

Directions: 10am-6pm (last entries 5pm) Tues-Sun during term times and every day during school holidays and Bank Holidays.

EXMOOR FALCONRY & ANIMAL FARM
Allerford, Near Porlock, Minehead,
Somerset TA24 8HJ
Tel: 01643 862816
e-mail: exmoor.falcon@virgin.net
www.exmoorfalconry.co.uk

READERS' OFFER 2008

10% off entry to Falconry Centre
Valid during 2008

NOT TO BE USED IN CONJUNCTION WITH ANY OTHER OFFER

FLEET AIR ARM MUSEUM
RNAS Yeovilton, Ilchester,
Somerset BA22 8HT
Tel: 01935 840565
e-mail: enquiries@fleetairarm.com
www.fleetairarm.com

READERS' OFFER 2008

One child FREE with full paying adult
Valid during 2008 except Bank Holidays

NOT TO BE USED IN CONJUNCTION WITH ANY OTHER OFFER

THE HELICOPTER MUSEUM
The Heliport, Locking Moor Road,
Weston-Super-Mare BS24 8PP
Tel: 01934 635227• Fax: 01934 645230
e-mail: helimuseum@btconnect.com
www.helicoptermuseum.co.uk

READERS' OFFER 2008

One child FREE with two full-paying adults
Valid from April to October 2008

NOT TO BE USED IN CONJUNCTION WITH ANY OTHER OFFER

YESTERDAY'S WORLD
High Street, Battle, E. Sussex TN33 0AQ
Tel: 01424 775378 (24hr info)
Enquiries/bookings: 01424 893938
e-mail: info@yesterdaysworld.co.uk
www.yesterdaysworld.co.uk

READERS' OFFER 2008

One child FREE when accompanied by one
full-paying adult. Valid until end 2008

NOT TO BE USED IN CONJUNCTION WITH ANY OTHER OFFER

Falconry centre with animals - flying displays, animal handling, feeding and bottle feeding - in 15th century NT farmyard setting on Exmoor. Also falconry and outdoor activities, hawk walks and riding.

Open: 10.30am to 5pm daily

Directions: A39 west of Minehead, turn right at Allerford, half a mile along lane on left.

Europe's largest naval aviation collection with over 40 aircraft on display , including Concorde 002 and Ark Royal Aircraft Carrier Experience. Situated on an operational naval air station.

Open: open daily April to October 10am-5.30pm; November to March 10am-4.30pm (closed Mon and Tues).

Directions: just off A303/A37 on B3151 at Ilchester. Yeovil rail station 10 miles.

The world's largest helicopter collection - over 70 exhibits, includes two royal helicopters, Russian Gunship and Vietnam veterans plus many award-winning exhibits. Cafe, shop. Flights.

PETS MUST BE KEPT UNDER CONTROL

Open: Wednesday to Sunday 10am to 5.30pm. Daily during school Easter and Summer holidays and Bank Holiday Mondays. November to March: 10am to 4.30pm

Directions: Junction 21 off M5 then follow the propellor signs.

The past is brought to life at one of the South East's best loved family attractions. 100,000+ nostalgic artefacts, set in a charming 15th century house and country garden. New attractions and tearooms.

Open: 9.30am to 6pm (last admission 4.45pm, one hour earlier in winter). Closing times may vary – phone or check website.

Directions: just off A21 in Battle High Street opposite the Abbey.

29

PARADISE PARK & GARDENS
Avis Road, Newhaven,
East Sussex BN9 0DH
Tel: 01273 512123 • Fax: 01273 616000
e-mail: enquiries@paradisepark.co.uk
www.paradisepark.co.uk

READERS' OFFER 2008

*Admit one FREE child with one adult
paying full entrance price. Valid during 2008*

NOT TO BE USED IN CONJUNCTION WITH ANY OTHER OFFER

WILDERNESS WOOD
Hadlow Down, Near Uckfield,
East Sussex TN22 4HJ
Tel: 01825 830509• Fax: 01825 830977
e-mail: enquiries@wildernesswood.co.uk
www.wildernesswood.co.uk

READERS' OFFER 2008

*one FREE admission with a full-paying adult
Valid during 2008 (not for Special Events/Bank Holidays)*

NOT TO BE USED IN CONJUNCTION WITH ANY OTHER OFFER

EARNLEY BUTTERFLIES & GARDENS
133 Almodington Lane, Earnley, Chichester,
West Sussex PO20 7JR
Tel: 01243 512637
e-mail: earnleygardens@msn.com
www.earnleybutterfliesandgardens.co.uk

READERS' OFFER 2008

*£2 per person offer normal entry prices.
Valid late March to end October 2008.*

NOT TO BE USED IN CONJUNCTION WITH ANY OTHER OFFER

STRATFORD BUTTERFLY FARM
Swan's Nest Lane, Stratford-upon-Avon
Warwickshire CV37 7LS
Tel: 01789 299288 • Fax: 01789 415878
e-mail: sales@butterflyfarm.co.uk
www.butterflyfarm.co.uk

READERS' OFFER 2008

*Admit TWO for the price of ONE
Valid until 31/12/2008*

NOT TO BE USED IN CONJUNCTION WITH ANY OTHER OFFER

Discover 'Planet Earth' for an unforgettable experience. A unique Museum of Life, Dinosaur Safari, beautiful Water Gardens with fish and wildfowl, plant houses, themed gardens, Heritage Trail, miniature railway. Playzone includes crazy golf and adventure play areas. Garden Centre and Terrace Cafe.

Open: open daily, except Christmas Day and Boxing Day.

Directions: signposted off A26 and A259.

Wilderness Wood is a unique family-run working woodland park in the Sussex High Weald. Explore trails and footpaths, enjoy local cakes and ices, try the adventure playground. Many special events and activities. Parties catered for. Green Tourism Gold Award.

Open: daily 10am to 5.30pm or dusk if earlier.

Directions: on the south side of the A272 in the village of Hadlow Down. Signposted with a brown tourist sign.

3 attractions in 1. Tropical butterflies, exotic animals of many types in our Noah's Ark Rescue Centre. Theme gardens with a free competition for kids. Rejectamenta - the nostalgia museum.

Open: 10am - 6pm daily late March to end October.

Directions: signposted from A27/A286 junction at Chichester.

Wander through a tropical rainforest with a myriad of multicoloured butterflies, sunbirds and koi carp. See fascinating animals in Insect City and view deadly spiders in perfect safety in Arachnoland.

Open: daily except Christmas Day. 10am-6pm summer, 10am-dusk winter.

Directions: on south bank of River Avon opposite Royal Shakespeare Theatre. Easily accessible from town centre, 5 minutes' walk.

31

FHG READERS' OFFER 2008

HATTON FARM VILLAGE AT HATTON COUNTRY WORLD
Dark Lane, Hatton, Near Warwick,
Warwickshire CV35 8XA
Tel: 01926 843411
e-mail: hatton@hattonworld.com
www.hattonworld.com

Admit one child FREE with one full-paying adult day ticket. Valid during 2008 except Bank Holidays or for entrance to Santa's Grotto promotion.

NOT TO BE USED IN CONJUNCTION WITH ANY OTHER OFFER

FHG READERS' OFFER 2008

AVONCROFT MUSEUM
Stoke Heath,
Bromsgrove,
Worcestershire B60 4JR
Tel: 01527 831363 • Fax: 01527 876934
www.avoncroft.org.uk

One FREE child with one full-paying adult
Valid from March to November 2008

NOT TO BE USED IN CONJUNCTION WITH ANY OTHER OFFER

FHG READERS' OFFER 2008

EMBSAY & BOLTON ABBEY STEAM RAILWAY
Bolton Abbey Station, Skipton,
North Yorkshire BD23 6AF
Tel: 01756 710614
e-mail: embsay.steam@btinternet.com
www.embsayboltonabbeyrailway.org.uk

One adult travels FREE when accompanied by a full fare paying adult (does not include Special Event days). Valid during 2008.

NOT TO BE USED IN CONJUNCTION WITH ANY OTHER OFFER

FHG READERS' OFFER 2008

WORLD OF JAMES HERRIOT
23 Kirkgate, Thirsk,
North Yorkshire YO7 1PL
Tel: 01845 524234
Fax: 01845 525333
www.worldofjamesherriot.org

Admit TWO for the price of ONE (one voucher per transaction only). Valid until October 2008

NOT TO BE USED IN CONJUNCTION WITH ANY OTHER OFFER

32

Hatton Farm Village offers a wonderful mix of farmyard animals, adventure play, shows, demonstrations, and events, all set in the stunning Warwickshire countryside.

Open: daily 10am-5pm (4pm during winter). Closed Christmas Day and Boxing Day.

Directions: 5 minutes from M40 (J15), A46 towards Coventry, then just off A4177 (follow brown tourist signs).

FHG GUIDES, ABBEY MILL BUSINESS CENTRE, PAISLEY PA1 1TJ • www.holidayguides.com

A fascinating world of historic buildings covering 7 centuries, rescued and rebuilt on an open-air site in the heart of the Worcestershire countryside.

PETS ON LEADS ONLY

Open: July and August all week. March to November varying times, please telephone for details.

Directions: A38 south of Bromsgrove, near Junction 1 of M42, Junction 5 of M5.

FHG GUIDES, ABBEY MILL BUSINESS CENTRE, PAISLEY PA1 1TJ • www.holidayguides.com

Steam trains operate over a 4½ mile line from Bolton Abbey Station to Embsay Station. Many family events including Thomas the Tank Engine take place during major Bank Holidays.

Open: steam trains run every Sunday throughout the year and up to 7 days a week in summer. 10.30am to 4.30pm

Directions: Embsay Station signposted from the A59 Skipton by-pass; Bolton Abbey Station signposted from the A59 at Bolton Abbey.

FHG GUIDES, ABBEY MILL BUSINESS CENTRE, PAISLEY PA1 1TJ • www.holidayguides.com

Visit James Herriot's original house recreated as it was in the 1940s. Television sets used in the series 'All Creatures Great and Small'. There is a children's interactive gallery with life-size model farm animals and three rooms dedicated to the history of veterinary medicine.

Open: daily. Easter-Oct 10am-5pm; Nov-Easter 11am to 4pm

Directions: follow signs off A1 or A19 to Thirsk, then A168, off Thirsk market place

FHG GUIDES, ABBEY MILL BUSINESS CENTRE, PAISLEY PA1 1TJ • www.holidayguides.com

Visit the FHG website
www.holidayguides.com
for details of the wide choice of accommodation
featured in the full range of FHG titles

All types of birds of prey exhibited here, from owls and kestrels to eagles and vultures. Special flying displays 12 noon, 1.30pm and 3pm. Bird handling courses arranged for either half or full days.

GUIDE DOGS ONLY

Open: 10am to 4.30pm summer 10am to 4pm winter

Directions: on main A65 trunk road outside Settle. Follow brown direction signs.

FHG GUIDES, ABBEY MILL BUSINESS CENTRE, PAISLEY PA1 1TJ • www.holidayguides.com

Dinostar features an exhibition of dinosaurs and fossils. Highlights include a T-Rex skull, Triceratops bones you can touch, and our unique dinosaur sound box.

Open: 11am to 5pm Wednesday to Sunday.

Directions: in the Fruit Market area of Hull's Old Town, close to The Deep and Hull Marina.

FHG GUIDES, ABBEY MILL BUSINESS CENTRE, PAISLEY PA1 1TJ • www.holidayguides.com

A fascinating display of railway carriages and a wide range of railway items telling the story of rail travel over the years.

ALL PETS MUST BE KEPT ON LEADS

Open: daily 11am to 4.30pm

Directions: approximately one mile from Keighley on A629 Halifax road. Follow brown tourist signs

FHG GUIDES, ABBEY MILL BUSINESS CENTRE, PAISLEY PA1 1TJ • www.holidayguides.com

Please note

All the information in this book is given in good faith in the belief that it is correct. However, the publishers cannot guarantee the facts given in these pages, neither are they responsible for changes in policy, ownership or terms that may take place after the date of going to press. Readers should always satisfy themselves that the facilities they require are available and that the terms, if quoted, still apply.

 **READERS' OFFER 2008**

STORYBOOK GLEN
Maryculter,
Aberdeen
Aberdeenshire AB12 5FT
Tel: 01224 732941
www.storybookglenaberdeen.co.uk

10% discount on all admissions
Valid until end 2008

NOT TO BE USED IN CONJUNCTION WITH ANY OTHER OFFER

 **READERS' OFFER 2008**

THE GRASSIC GIBBON CENTRE
Arbuthnott, Laurencekirk,
Aberdeenshire AB30 1PB
Tel: 01561 361668
e-mail: lgginfo@grassicgibbon.com
www.grassicgibbon.com

TWO for the price of ONE entry to exhibition (based on full adult rate only). Valid during 2008 (not groups)

NOT TO BE USED IN CONJUNCTION WITH ANY OTHER OFFER

 **READERS' OFFER 2008**

INVERARAY JAIL
Church Square, Inveraray,
Argyll PA32 8TX
Tel: 01499 302381• Fax: 01499 302195
e-mail: info@inverarayjail.co.uk
www.inverarayjail.co.uk

One child FREE with one full-paying adult
Valid until end 2008

NOT TO BE USED IN CONJUNCTION WITH ANY OTHER OFFER

 **READERS' OFFER 2008**

SCOTTISH MARITIME MUSEUM
Harbourside, Irvine,
Ayrshire KA12 8QE
Tel: 01294 278283
Fax: 01294 313211
www.scottishmaritimemuseum.org

TWO for the price of ONE
Valid from April to October 2008

NOT TO BE USED IN CONJUNCTION WITH ANY OTHER OFFER

28-acre theme park with over 100 nursery rhyme characters, set in beautifully landscaped gardens. Shop and restaurant on site.

Open: 1st March to 31st October: daily 10am to 6pm; 1st Nov to end Feb: Sat/Sun only 11am to 4pm

Directions: 6 miles west of Aberdeen off B9077

Visitor Centre dedicated to the much-loved Scottish writer Lewis Grassic Gibbon. Exhibition, cafe, gift shop. Outdoor children's play area. Disabled access throughout.

Open: daily April to October 10am to 4.30pm. Groups by appointment including evenings.

Directions: on the B967, accessible and signposted from both A90 and A92.

19th century prison with fully restored 1820 courtroom and two prisons. Guides in uniform as warders, prisoners and matron. Remember your camera!

Open: April to October 9.30am-6pm (last admission 5pm); November to March 10am-5pm (last admission 4pm)

Directions: A83 to Campbeltown

Scotland's seafaring heritage is among the world's richest and you can relive the heyday of Scottish shipping at the Maritime Museum.

Open: 1st April to 31st October - 10am-5pm

Directions: situated on Irvine harbourside and only a 10 minute walk from Irvine train station.

The wild animal conservation centre of Southern Scotland. A varied collection of over 150 animals from all over the world can be seen within natural woodland settings.
Picnic areas, cafe/gift shop, outdoor play area, woodland walks, close animal encounters.

Open: 10am to dusk 1st February to 30 November.

Directions: follow brown tourist signs from A75; one mile from Kirkcudbright on the B727.

Visitors can experience the thrill of a guided tour into an 18thC lead mine, explore the two period cottages, visit the second oldest subscription library and investigate the Visitor & Exhibition Centre. Taster sessions of gold panning available July and August.

Open: 1 April - 30 June: 11am-4.30pm July, August and Bank Holidays: 10am -5pm.

Directions: off M74. J14 if travelling north, J13 if travelling south.

A fantastic display of gems, crystals, minerals and fossils. An experience you'll treasure forever. Gift shop, tearoom and AV display.

Open: Summer - 9.30am to 5.30pm daily; Winter - 10am to 4pm daily. Closed Christmas to end January.

Directions: follow signs from A75 Dumfries/Stranraer.

Indoor adventure play area, farm park, toyshop and cafe. A great day out for all the family, with sledge and zip slides, mini-golf, trampolines, bumper boats, pottery painting and so much more.

Open: Monday to Saturday 10am-5.30pm.

Directions: just off the A75/A701 roundabout heading for Moffat and Edinburgh.

THE SCOTTISH MINING MUSEUM
Lady Victoria Colliery, Newtongrange,
Midlothian EH22 4QN
Tel: 0131-663 7519 • Fax: 0131-654 0952
visitorservices@scottishminingmuseum.com
www.scottishminingmuseum.com

One child FREE with full-paying adult
Valid January to December 2008

K·U·P·E·R·A·R·D
READERS' OFFER 2008

NOT TO BE USED IN CONJUNCTION WITH ANY OTHER OFFER

BUTTERFLY & INSECT WORLD
Dobbies Garden World, Melville Nursery,
Lasswade, Midlothian EH18 1AZ
Tel: 0131-663 4932 • Fax: 0131-654 2774
e-mail: info@edinburgh-butterfly-world.co.uk
www.edinburgh-butterfly-world.co.uk

One child FREE with full paying adult.
Valid during 2008.

K·U·P·E·R·A·R·D
READERS' OFFER 2008

NOT TO BE USED IN CONJUNCTION WITH ANY OTHER OFFER

BO'NESS & KINNEIL RAILWAY
Bo'ness Station, Union Street,
Bo'ness, West Lothian EH51 9AQ
Tel: 01506 822298
e-mail: enquiries.railway@srps.org.uk
www.srps.org.uk

FREE child train fare with one paying adult/concession. Valid 29th March-26th Oct 2008. Not Thomas events or Santa Steam trains

K·U·P·E·R·A·R·D
READERS' OFFER 2008

NOT TO BE USED IN CONJUNCTION WITH ANY OTHER OFFER

MYRETON MOTOR MUSEUM
Aberlady,
East Lothian
EH32 0PZ
Tel: 01875 870288

MYRETON MOTOR MUSEUM

One child FREE with each paying adult
Valid during 2008

K·U·P·E·R·A·R·D
READERS' OFFER 2008

NOT TO BE USED IN CONJUNCTION WITH ANY OTHER OFFER

visitscotland 5-Star Attraction with two floors of interactive exhibitions, a 'Magic Helmet' tour of the pithead, re-created coal road and coal face, and new Big Stuff tour. Largest working winding engine in Britain.

Open: daily. Summer: 10am to 5pm (last tour 3.30pm). Winter: 10am to 4pm (last tour 2.30pm)

Directions: 5 minutes from Sherrifhall Roundabout on Edinburgh City Bypass on A7 south

See free-flying exotic butterflies in a tropical rainforest paradise, iguanas roaming free in jungle flora, and small birds darting in and out of the flowers. Have close encounters of the crawly kind in the 'Bugs & Beasties' exhibition that includes arrow frogs, tarantulas, amazing leaf-cutter ants and a unique Scottish Honey Bee display.

Open: daily. 9.30am-5.30pm summer, 10am-5pm winter.

Directions: located just off the Edinburgh City Bypass at the Gilmerton exit or Sherrifhall roundabout.

Steam and heritage diesel passenger trains from Bo'ness to Birkhill for guided tours of Birkhill fireclay mines. Explore the history of Scotland's railways in the Scottish Railway Exhibition. Coffee shop and souvenir shop.

Open: weekends Easter to October, daily July and August.

Directions: in the town of Bo'ness. Leave M9 at Junction 3 or 5, then follow brown tourist signs.

On show is a large collection, from 1899, of cars, bicycles, motor cycles and commercials. There is also a large collection of period advertising, posters and enamel signs.

Open: March-November - open daily 11am to 4pm. December-February - weekends 11am to 3pm or by special appointment.

Directions: off A198 near Aberlady. Two miles from A1.

41

CLYDEBUILT SCOTTISH MARITIME MUSEUM
Braehead Shopping Centre, King's Inch Road,
Glasgow G51 4BN
Tel: 0141-886 1013 • Fax: 0141-886 1015
e-mail: clydebuilt@scotmaritime.org.uk
www.scottishmaritimemuseum.org

READERS' OFFER 2008

HALF PRICE admission for up to 4 persons.
Valid during 2008.

NOT TO BE USED IN CONJUNCTION WITH ANY OTHER OFFER

SPEYSIDE HEATHER GARDEN & VISITOR CENTRE
Speyside Heather Centre, Dulnain Bridge,
Inverness-shire PH26 3PA
Tel: 01479 851359 • Fax: 01479 851396
e-mail: enquiries@heathercentre.com
www.heathercentre.com

READERS' OFFER 2008

FREE entry to 'Heather Story' exhibition
Valid during 2008

NOT TO BE USED IN CONJUNCTION WITH ANY OTHER OFFER

LLANBERIS LAKE RAILWAY
Gilfach Ddu, Llanberis,
Gwynedd LL55 4TY
Tel: 01286 870549
e-mail: info@lake-railway.co.uk
www.lake-railway.co.uk

READERS' OFFER 2008

One pet travels FREE with each full fare paying adult
Valid Easter to October 2008

NOT TO BE USED IN CONJUNCTION WITH ANY OTHER OFFER

ANIMALARIUM
Borth,
Ceredigion
SY24 5NA
Tel: 01970 871224
www.animalarium.co.uk

READERS' OFFER 2008

FREE child with full paying adult.
Valid during 2008.

NOT TO BE USED IN CONJUNCTION WITH ANY OTHER OFFER

The story of Glasgow and the River Clyde brought vividly to life using AV, hands-on and interactive techniques. You can navigate your own ship, safely load your cargo, operate an engine, and go aboard the 130-year-old coaster 'Kyles'. Ideal for kids young and old wanting an exciting day out. New - The Clyde's Navy.

Open: 10am to 5.30pm daily

Directions: Green Car Park near M&S at Braehead Shopping Centre.

Award-winning attraction with unique 'Heather Story' exhibition, gallery, giftshop, large garden centre selling 300 different heathers, antique shop, children's play area and famous Clootie Dumpling restaurant.

Open: all year except Christmas Day.

Directions: just off A95 between Aviemore and Grantown-on-Spey.

A 60-minute ride along the shores of beautiful Padarn Lake behind a quaint historic steam engine. Magnificent views of the mountains from lakeside picnic spots.

DOGS MUST BE KEPT ON LEAD AT ALL TIMES ON TRAIN

Open: most days Easter to October. Free timetable leaflet on request.

Directions: just off A4086 Caernarfon to Capel Curig road at Llanberis; follow 'Country Park' signs.

A collection of unusual and interesting animals, including breeding pairs and colonies of exotic and endangered species whose natural environment is under threat. Many were unwanted exotic pets or came from other zoos.

Open: 10am - 6pm April to October

Directions: only a short walk from the railway station and beach in Borth, which lies between Aberystwyth and Machynlleth.

43

Visit the FHG website
www.holidayguides.com
for details of the wide choice of accommodation

featured in the full range of FHG titles

Mini-rainforest full of tropical plants and exotic butterflies. Personal attention of the owner, Mr John Devereux. Gift shop, cafe, video room, exhibition. Suitable for disabled visitors. VisitWales Quality Assured Visitor Attraction.

PETS NOT ALLOWED IN TROPICAL HOUSE ONLY

Open: daily Easter to end October 10.30am to 5pm

Directions: West Wales, 7 miles north of Cardigan off Aberystwyth road. Follow brown tourist signs on A487.

FHG GUIDES, ABBEY MILL BUSINESS CENTRE, PAISLEY PA1 1TJ • www.holidayguides.com

Journey through the lanes of cycle history and see bicycles from Boneshakers and Penny Farthings up to modern Raleigh cycles. Over 250 machines on display

PETS MUST BE KEPT ON LEADS

Open: 1st March to 1st November daily 10am onwards.

Directions: brown signs to car park. Town centre attraction.

FHG GUIDES, ABBEY MILL BUSINESS CENTRE, PAISLEY PA1 1TJ • www.holidayguides.com

Make a pit stop whatever the weather! Join an ex-miner on a tour of discovery, ride the cage to pit bottom and take a thrilling ride back to the surface. Multi-media presentations, period village street, children's adventure play area, restaurant and gift shop. Disabled access with assistance.

Open: Open daily 10am to 6pm (last tour 4pm). Closed Mondays Oct - Easter, also Dec 25th to early Jan.

Directions: Exit Junction 32 M4, signposted from A470 Pontypridd. Trehafod is located between Pontypridd and Porth.

FHG GUIDES, ABBEY MILL BUSINESS CENTRE, PAISLEY PA1 1TJ • www.holidayguides.com

Please note

All the information in this book is given in good faith in the belief that it is correct. However, the publishers cannot guarantee the facts given in these pages, neither are they responsible for changes in policy, ownership or terms that may take place after the date of going to press. Readers should always satisfy themselves that the facilities they require are available and that the terms, if quoted, still apply.

Guide to Good Beaches

How can I find a good, clean beach?
Can I take my dog on the beach?
How do I know the water is safe to swim in?

Britain has hundreds of beautiful beaches, many peaceful and secluded, others with lots of facilities which make them popular with families.

There are five beach scheme awards , and if you contact them or have a look at their websites, you will find lots of information on what is the best one for you and your family.

Started in 1987 as part of the EEC's Year of the Environment, the **BLUE FLAG** campaign aims not only to encourage and reward high standards of beach management at coastal resorts, but also to promote improved quality of bathing water. It is awarded in over 23 countries in Europe and South Africa for resort beaches and marinas with high standards of environmental management. To win a Blue Flag, therefore, water quality is judged along with cleanliness and beach facilities. A dog ban during the summer is an absolute requirement and only beaches regularly used by the public, and resorts with safe bathing all year round may enter the competition. In 2007 137 beaches in Britain were awarded the coveted Blue Flag Award. ENCAMS (Keep Britain Tidy Group) co-ordinates the scheme in England, while Keep Scotland Tidy, Keep Wales Tidy and Tidy Northern Ireland oversee the scheme in their respective countries.

ENCAMS (Environmental Campaigns) is a part-government funded charity working for the improvement of local environments. Its aims are to encourage individual,  corporate and community responsibility for care of the environment through a variety of campaigns and programmes. All of the award-winning beaches have met very strict criteria, which include meeting the EC requirements for bathing water, providing good beach safety and supervision, putting in place good beach management (including dog controls and facilities for disabled visitors) and providing the public with clear information. A large database of UK beaches is maintained, with information on water quality, access, safety, cleanliness, dog control, first aid provision and conservation management.

 In England the Encams Quality Coast Award recognises different types of beach, and the website can be searched by region to find the perfect one for you.

In Scotland, Wales and Northern Ireland, Seaside Awards are presented annually for well maintained and managed resort and rural beaches, where bathing water quality must achieve the EC mandatory standard.

 Green Coast Award is run by Keep Wales Tidy and is given to unspoilt rural beaches in Wales and the Republic of Ireland for high water quality and best practice in environmental management. It places a great emphasis on community and environmental activities, and is intended to promote and protect rural beaches. Bathing water must achieve the EC Guideline standard.

The Marine Conservation Society produces a list of 'recommended' beaches which have the highest standards of bathing water quality. This award only addresses water quality and lists beaches which pose a minimum risk of sewage contamination and related diseases.

The Good Beach Guide (online www.goodbeachguide.co.uk) is a searchable database of 1200 beaches in the UK and Ireland, each with description, photo and map.

How to find out more:
Blue Flag Beaches • www.blueflag.org.uk
ENCAMS • www.encams.org
Seaside Awards • www.keepscotlandbeautiful.org
Green Coast Award • www.keepwalestidy.org
Marine Conservation Society • www.mcsuk.org

EUROPEAN
BLUE FLAG Beaches
in Britain and Northern Ireland
2007

Scotland
- Dundee & Angus
- Fife

Northern Ireland
- Londonderry
- Antrim • Co. Down

North East England
- Tyne & Wear
- East Yorkshire
- North Yorkshire

Midlands
- Lincolnshire

Wales
- Anglesey • Gwynedd
- North Wales
- Carmarthenshire
- Ceredigion
- Pembrokeshire
- South Wales

East England
- Norfolk • Suffolk
- Essex

South West England
- Cornwall • Dorset • Devon

South East England
Hampshire • Kent • East Sussex
• West Sussex • Isle of Wight

The beach at Rhyl, North Wales

Cornwall
Crooklets
Gyllyngvase
Porthtowan
Polzeath
Sennen Cove
Carbis Bay
Marazion
Porthmeor
Porthminster

North Devon
Woolacombe Sands
Croyde Bay
Westward Ho!
Ilfracombe Tunnels

South Devon
Bantham
Bigbury on Sea
Blackpool Sands
Challaborough
Dawlish Warren
Salcombe South Sands
Sandy Bay
Torbay
  Breakwater
  Broadsands
  Goodrington South
  Meadfoot
  Oddicombe

Dorset
Poole
  Canford Cliffs
  Branksome Chine
  Sandbanks
  Shore Road
Bournemouth
  Fisherman's Walk
  Alum Chine
  Durley Chine
  Southbourne
Swanage Central

Hampshire
West Beachlands Central
West Beachlands West

Sussex
Bognor Regis
Hove Lawns
Eastbourne
West Wittering
West Street

Kent
Birchington Minnis Bay
Botany Bay
Herne Bay
West Bay Westgate
St Mildred's Bay
Stone Bay, Broadstairs
Westbrook Margate
Tankerton
Margate Main Sands

Isle of Wight
Ryde East
Sandown
Shanklin

Norfolk
Great Yarmouth Gorleston
Cromer
Mundesley
Sea Palling
Sheringham

Essex
Southend Three Shells
Shoebury Common
Shoeburyness
Brightlingsea
Dovercourt

Suffolk
Felixstowe South
Lowestoft North
Lowestoft South
Southwold Pier

Lincolnshire
Cleethorpes
Mablethorpe Central
Skegness Central
Sutton on Sea Central

Tyne & Wear
Whitley Bay South
Tynemouth
  King Edwards Bay
  Longsands South
Roker
Seaburn
Sandhaven
Seaton Carew

East Yorkshire
Bridlington North
Bridlington South
Hornsea
Withernsea

North Yorkshire
Scarborough North
Filey
Whitby

WALES

Gwynedd
Pwllheli
Fairbourne
Tywyn
Abersoch
Dinas Dinlle
Barmouth Abermaw

Anglesey
Benllech
Llanddona
Llanddwyn
Porth Dafarch
Trearddur Bay

North Wales
Llandudno North Shore
Llandudno West Shore
Penmaenmawr
Prestatyn Central

Ceredigion
Borth
New Quay
Tresaith
Aberystwyth North
Aberystwyth South

Carmarthenshire
Pembrey Country Park
Pendine

Pembrokeshire
Dale
Broadhaven North
Lydstep
Newgale
Poppit Sands
Saundersfoot
St Davids Whitesands
Tenby Castle
Tenby North
Tenby South

South Wales
Porthcawl Rest Bay
Barry, Whitmore Bay
Bracelet Bay
Caswell Bay
Langland Bay
Port Eynon
Trecco Bay

SCOTLAND

Dundee & Angus
Montrose

Fife
Aberdour Silver Sands
Burntisland
Elie Harbour
St Andrews West

NORTHERN IRELAND
Ballycastle
Cranfield
Magilligan/Benone Strand
Portrush East
Portrush West
Portrush White Rocks
Portstewart
Tyrella

FREE AND REDUCED RATE HOLIDAY VISITS!
Don't miss our READERS' OFFER VOUCHERS
on pages 9-44

CORNWALL

 Best Beaches

Several beaches which meet the strict criteria of the European Foundation for Environmental Education have been awarded a prestigious Blue Flag.

BLUE FLAG BEACHES 2007
- *Polzeath*
- *Carbis Bay*
- *Crooklets*
- *Marazion*
- *St Ives Porthmeor*
- *St Ives Porthminster*
- *Sennen Cove*
- *Gyllyngvase*
- *Porthtowan*

[i] South West Tourism
(Bristol & Bath, Cornwall, Devon, Dorset, Gloucestershire & The Cotswolds, Somerset, Wiltshire).

- Tel: 0870 442 0880
- Fax: 0870 442 0881
- e-mail: post@swtourism.co.uk
- www.visitsouthwest.co.uk

For more information about holidaying in Cornwall see:
- www.cornwalltouristboard.co.uk • 01872 322900
- www.cata.co.uk (Cornwall Association of Tourist Attractions)
- www.secta.org.uk (South East Cornwall)
- www.northcornwall-live.com (North Cornwall)
- www.go-cornwall.com (West Cornwall)

BUDE

⚒ **Family Fun Activities:** Seawater swimming pool on Summerleaze beach • Tropical Leisure Pool, including flume and wave machine, fitness suite, 10-pin bowling, roller blading rink and indoor adventure play area • Adventure centres offering tuition in various sports • Sports hall, multi-gym and activities • Sustrans cycle route • Bude Canal Wharf area • Heritage Trail • Museum • Mini-golf, putting, golf, bowls, squash, table tennis, cricket, tennis, sea and canal angling.

☆ **Special Events: May:** Model Boat Festival; re-enactment of Battle of Stamford Hill. **May-September:** events, shows, fetes and revels. **July:** Bude festival of Music, Downhill Classic Triathlon. **August:** arts & crafts exhibitions; Bude Carnival Week; Lifeboat Week; 8-day Bude Jazz Festival. **September:** Quadrathon. **October:** canoe sprint.

ⓘ **Bude Visitor Centre, The Crescent, Bude EX23 8LE • 01288 354240 e-mail: budetic@visitbude.info www.visitbude.info**

🏖 **Beaches**

• SUMMERLEAZE BEACH. Level access via car park. *Safety and maintenance:* lifeguards during summer months. *Beach facilities:* beach huts, deck chairs etc for hire; mini-golf and go karts; open sea pool; cafe, shop and restaurant; RNLI centre/shop. Toilets, & access. *Dog restrictions:* none, but they must be kept under proper control.

• CROOKLETS BEACH. Sandy, with level access. Car park adjoining. *Safety and maintenance:* lifeguards on duty during June/July/August. *Beach facilities:* deckchairs, beach huts, windbreaks etc for hire; snack bar and beach shop; toilets (disabled facilities for members of National Radar Key Scheme). *Dog restrictions:* banned from beach area from Good Friday to 1st October.

• SANDY MOUTH BEACH. Beach owned by National Trust. *Safety and maintenance:* lifeguards during summer months. *Beach facilities:* cafe owned by NT. Toilets but no & facilities. *Dog restrictions:* none.

NEWQUAY

⚒ **Family Fun Activities:** Tunnels Through Time • Dairyland • Cornwall Pearl • Trerice Manor • Trenance Park with Water World fun pool and Newquay Zoo • Blue Reef Aquarium • Tennis, golf, pitch and putt, miniature railway, lakeside cafe, boating, sailing, surfing (Fistral Beach), angling, golf course • Discos, nightclubs.

☆ **Special Events: June:** Newquay Surf Triathlon. **July:** Surf Festival, Newquay Harbour Sports. **August:** British Surfing Championships. Gig racing.

ⓘ **Tourist Information Centre, Marcus Hill, Newquay • 01637 854020 www.newquay.org.uk**

🏖 **Beaches**

• HARBOUR BEACH. Sandy and naturally sheltered; promenade and limited parking. *Safety and maintenance:* cleaned daily. *Beach facilities:* pleasure craft; fishing and shark trips; ice cream kiosk; restaurant; toilets with & access.

• TOWAN BEACH. 400 yards long, sandy with rock pools, naturally sheltered promenade. & access. Parking 5 minutes' walk. *Safety and maintenance:* flagged, warning signs, lifeguards; cleaned daily. *Beach facilities:* deck chairs, windbreaks, wet suits; ice-cream kiosk, snack bar.

• GREAT WESTERN BEACH. 200 yards long, sandy with rock pools and cliffs; parking 5 minutes' walk. *Safety and maintenance:* flagged, warning signs, lifeguards; cleaned daily. *Beach facilities:* deck chairs, windbreaks, surfboards; ice cream and snack bar; toilets with & access.

53

- TOLCARNE BEACH. 500 yards long, sandy. Access down cliff steps, also path to beach. Parking 6 minutes' walk. *Safety and maintenance:* flagged, warning signs; cleaned daily. *Beach facilities:* deck chairs, surfboards, beach huts, trampolines; ice-cream kiosks, cafeteria, beach shop, barbecues; toilets.

- LUSTY GLAZE BEACH. 200 yards long; sandy with cliffs and rock pools, access via steps. *Safety and maintenance:* flagged, warning signs, lifeguards; cleaned daily. *Beach facilities:* deck chairs, surf boards, beach huts; ice-cream kiosk, cafe/takeaway, pub/restaurant and beach shop; showers and toilets; outdoor adventure centre. *Dog restrictions:* banned between 8am and 7pm.

- PORTH BEACH. 300 yards long, sandy and naturally sheltered with rock pools. Good parking. *Safety and maintenance:* flagged, warning signs, lifeguards; cleaned daily. *Beach facilities:* deck chairs, boogie boards, windbreaks; ice-cream kiosks, snack bars, restaurant and pub. *Dog restrictions:* banned from Easter to end September.

- WHIPSIDERRY BEACH. 200 yards long; sandy with cliffs and steps. *Safety and maintenance:* warning signs; cut off by tidal seas around cliffs.

- WATERGATE BEACH. Two miles long, sandy; good parking. *Safety and maintenance:* flagged, warning signs, lifeguards; cleaned daily. *Beach facilities:* surfboards; surf school and power kite school; bistro and takeaway, shops; toilets.

- CRANTOCK BEACH. Approx. one mile long, naturally sheltered with sandy dunes; good parking. *Safety and maintenance:* flagged, warning signs, lifeguards; Gannel tidal estuary very dangerous when tide going out. Beach owned and cleaned by NT. *Beach facilities:* deck chairs, surf boards; ice-cream kiosks, snack bars; toilets.

- FISTRAL BEACH. Approx. one mile long, sandy with dunes; good parking. *Safety and maintenance:* flagged, warning signs, lifeguards; cleaned daily. *Beach facilities:* deck chairs and windbreaks; wetsuit and surfboard hire; restaurant, cafe and takeaway, shops; toilets with & access.

PENZANCE

⛵ **Family Fun Activities:** Water sports area at Marazion • Sea water swimming pool, indoor swimming pool, children's playground, boating lake, amusement arcade • Riding, tennis, bowls, putting, go-karting • Shark fishing, sailing, sub-aqua, sea and fresh water angling • Rock climbing • Cinema, arts theatre, dance halls and discos, clubs and pub entertainment nightly.

☆ **Special Events: April:** British Funboard Cup, Hockey Festival. **June:** Golowan Festival. **August:** Newlyn Fish Festival. **September:** Michaelmas Fair.

ℹ️ **Tourist Information Centre, Station Road, Penzance TR18 2NF 01736 362207 www.go-cornwall.com**

ST IVES

⛵ **Family Fun Activities:** Boat trips, sea angling, sailing, surfing, parascending, tennis, bowling, squash, putting • Leisure centre with swimming pool and gym • Museum, art galleries (Tate St Ives).

ℹ️ **Tourist Information Centre, The Guildhall, St Ives TR26 2DS 01736 796297 www.stives-cornwall.co.uk**

🏖 Beaches

- PORTHMEOR BEACH. One km long, sand backed by low cliffs. Good surfing beach. Limited parking. *Safety and maintenance:* area for use of surfboards marked with buoys, lifeguards in summer months; cleaned daily during holiday season. *Beach facilities:* deck chairs, surf boards, beach huts for hire; boat trips around bay; beach shop and cafe on promenade; toilets. *Dog restrictions:* banned from Easter to 1st October.

☆ Fun for all the Family ☆

Colliford Lake Park, Bolventnor, Bodmin (01208 821469). Set amidst 50 acres of moorland beauty, rare breeds of animals and birds, craft demonstrations, adventure play areas. New '4 in 1' attraction.
www.collifordlakepark.com

Dairyland Farmworld, near Newquay (01872 510246). An all-weather attraction with fun for the whole family. Mini tractors, trampolines, assault course, farm park, pony rides, and lots, lots more
www.edenproject.com

Goonhilly Satellite Earth Station, near Helston (0800 679593). The fascinating world of satellite communications - see global TV live as it happens. Audio-visual show, conducted tours; shop, restaurant.
www.goonhilly.bt.com

Lappa Valley Railway and Leisure Park, St Newlyn East, Newquay (01872 510317). Two-mile ride on steam train, plus leisure area with crazy golf, adventure playground, boating lake, picnic areas, woodland walks.
www.lappavalley.co.uk

The Monkey Sanctuary, near Looe (01503 262532). Breeding colony of "Woolly" monkeys that enjoy the company of visitors!
www.monkeysanctuary.org

Land of Legend and Model Village , The Old Forge, Polperro (01503 272378). Exciting animated Land of Legend show detailing Cornish life; also model village.

Newquay Zoo, Trenance Leisure Park, Newquay (01637 873342). A wealth of wildlife including Tropical House, Children's Zoo, walk in Rabbit Warren; play areas; park with leisure facilities.
www.newquayzoo.co.uk

Paradise Park, near St Ives (01736 751020). Cornwall's conservation theme park which keeps and breeds endangered species.
www.paradisepark.org.uk

Poldark Mine and Heritage Complex, Wendron, Helston (01326 573173). An 18th century Cornish tin mine at 125 feet below ground level. Guided tours and working models; restaurant.
www.poldark-mine.co.uk

Shire Horse Farm and Carriage Museum, Treskillard, Redruth (01209 713606). See the shires at work on the farm and visit the blacksmith's shop. Guided tours, wagon rides; picnic area.

Tamar Otter Sanctuary, near Launceston (01566 785646). Enjoy a close encounter with these shy but playful creatures; also deer, owls and golden pheasants. Nature trail, tearoom and shop. No dogs.

Trinity House National Lighthouse Museum, Penzance (01736 360077). The world's finest collection of light house apparatus, illustrating their history and the lives of the keepers.
www.trinityhouse.co.uk

Tunnels Through Time, Newquay (01637 873379). More than 70 amazingly realistic characters re-create the stories and legends of Cornwall. Open Easter to October.
www.tunnelsthroughtime.co.uk

Wheal Martyn China Clay Heritage Centre, near St Austell (01726 850362). Restored 19th century clay works with working water wheels; nature trail and adventure trail.
www.wheal-martyn.com

Family-friendly hotel set in 4 acres of Cornish countryside

Wringford Down

Hat Lane, Cawsand, Cornwall PL10 1LE
Tel: 01752 822287

AA
★★★
Guest
Accommodation

accommodation@wringforddown.co.uk • www.cornwallholidays.co.uk

Located on the Rame peninsula in an Area of Outstanding Natural Beauty with tiny Cornish fishing villages, dramatic cliff top walks and secluded sandy bays.

- 11 suites, some within main building and others in adjacent chalets. All have private bathrooms.
- Well stocked bar, and restaurant serving excellent home-cooked food.
- Well equipped indoor and outdoor play areas with swings, slides, soft toys, ride-on toys, ball pool, playhouse etc; pool and table tennis tables for the older children. There is also a tennis court, which can be used for playing tennis, but which spends most of its time as a playground.
- Indoor pool and a smaller paddling pool, kept at a nicely warm 29 deg C. The pool is open from just before Easter until just after the October half term break.
- Television lounge and a playroom with books, board games and a piano.
- Courtyard room with a pool table and an adults-only room off the bar with a bar billiards table and dartboard.

In the old quiet part of Padstow and close to harbour, beaches and walks.
A beautiful small family-run hotel with personal friendly service and
comfortable accommodation of a very high standard. Non-smoking.
Eight en suite bedrooms. Off-street parking. Credit/debit cards accepted.

Tregea Hotel
16-18 High Street, Padstow, Cornwall PL28 8BB
Tel: 01841 532455 • Fax: 01841 533542
e-mail: enquiries@tregea.co.uk • www.tregea.co.uk

Penquite Farm
Golant, Fowey PL23 1LB

A stunning location in spectacular scenic
countryside offering wonderful river views
over the Fowey Valley. A perfect rural
retreat for a relaxing, enjoyable holiday
on a working farm, nestling beside a
beautiful 13th century church on the
edge of a peaceful riverside village.

A spacious, three-bedroom, split-level
house with two bathrooms, and two beautifully restored barn conversions, all rooms en

suite and tastefully furnished to a very high standard. Sleep four
(wheelchair-friendly), six and ten persons. All have own large gardens,
patio area, BBQs and ample parking. Ideal for touring, walking, beaches,
National Trust properties, gardens, and the Eden Project close by.

Ruth Varco • Tel & Fax: 01726 833319

ruth@penquitefarm.co.uk
www.penquitefarm.co.uk

FHG Guides
publish a large range of well-known accommodation guides.
We will be happy to send you details or you can use
the order form at the back of this book.

West Banbury Farm Cottages...where relaxation is a way of life
Come to West Banbury and you'll discover a rural haven where you can unwind and relax. We are in Broadwoodwidger, West Devon, ideally located for exploring Devon and Cornwall, with plenty of children's attractions within easy reach. We have ten charming cottages, all spacious and very comfortable, set around two courtyards with stunning views to Dartmoor. The cottages sleep 2 to 8. Large indoor pool, sauna, games room, children's play area, 9-hole pitch and putt, and a grass tennis court: plenty for the children to do in a safe environment. Dogs welcome. Short breaks are available.
For more information call **Amanda** on **01566 784946**
w w w . w e s t b a n b u r y . c o . u k

CHALETS • CARAVANS • CAMPING
St Ives Bay Holiday Park is set in sand dunes which run down to its own sandy beach. Many units have superb sea views. There is a large indoor pool and 2 clubs with FREE entertainment on the Park.

CALL OUR 24hr BROCHURE LINE
0800 317713
www.stivesbay.co.uk

FREE AND REDUCED RATE HOLIDAY VISITS!
Don't miss our
Readers' Offer Vouchers
on pages 9-44

BAMHAM FARM COTTAGES Higher Bamham Farm, Launceston PL15 9LD
Eight individually designed cottages, one mile from Launceston, the historic capital of Cornwall. The north and south coasts of Devon and Cornwall are easily accessible, as are Dartmoor and Bodmin Moor. Heated indoor swimming pool with paddling pool (open all year); games room. Video recorders and DVD players in cottages.

• Contact •
Richard and Jackie Chapman
Tel: 01566 772141
Fax: 01566 775266
e-mail: Jackie@bamhamfarm.co.uk
www.cottages-cornwall.co.uk

CUTKIVE WOOD HOLIDAY LODGES

Nestling in the heart of a peaceful and lovely family-owned country estate, there are six well-equipped cedar-clad lodges. Set on the edge of bluebell woods with wonderful rural views, you can relax and enjoy yourself in this tranquil and idyllic setting. Ideally situated to enjoy year-round holidays. You can help to feed the animals, milk the goats, explore the woods and fields. Big play area. So much to see and do - including memorable beaches, wonderful coasts, walk the moors, theme attractions, historic gems and the Eden Project. Dogs welcome. Short breaks. Open all year.

St Ive, Liskeard, Cornwall PL14 3ND • Tel: 01579 362216
www.cutkivewood.co.uk • holidays@cutkivewood.co.uk

Forget-Me-Not Farm Holidays

Situated on Trefranck, our 340-acre family-run beef and sheep farm, in North Cornwall, on the edge of enchanting Bodmin Moor and six miles from the spectacular North Cornwall Heritage Coast. We offer all year round luxury, 4-star, self-catering acccommodation.

Forget-Me-Not Cottage can comfortably sleep 6 and is tastefully decorated and superbly equipped, with a real log fire and central heating. **The Old Wagon House** is a stylish barn conversion and sleeps 2-4, with a 4-poster bed – ideal for romantic breaks. Mobility rating. **The Stable** is an en suite twin annexe to the Old Wagon House. **Honeysuckle Cottage** sleeps 6. Lovely views of the moor; beautiful garden. Well equipped. **Meadowsweet Cottage** - barn conversion, sleeps 4, surrounded by own woodlands. Abundance of wildlife. Excellent for cycling and walking holidays.

Trefranck is within easy reach of the Eden Project, the Lost Gardens of Heligan, Padstow and the Camel Trail.

Visit Bude, Crackington Haven, Padstow, Tintagel & The Eden Project.

**Trefranck Farm, St Clether, Launceston PL15 8QN
Mobile: 07790 453229
Tel: 01566 86284
e-mail: holidays@trefranck.co.uk
www.forget-me-not-farm-holidays.co.uk**

TREMAINE GREEN for MEMORABLE HOLIDAYS

"A beautiful private hamlet" of 11 traditional cosy Cornish craftsmen's cottages between **Looe** and **Polperro.** Clean, comfortable and well equipped, with a warm friendly atmosphere, for 2 to 8 people. Set in award-winning grounds, only 12 miles from the **Eden Project** with country and coastal walks nearby.

• Towels, Linen, Electric & Hot Water included • Dishwashers in larger cottages
• Launderette • Kids' Play Area • Games Room • Tennis Court • TV/DVDs • Wifi
• Cots & Highchairs • Pubs & Restaurants in easy walking distance • Activities Area

Mr & Mrs J Spreckley, Tremaine Green Country Cottages, Pelynt, Near Looe PL13 2LT

www.tremainegreen.co.uk • e-mail: stay@tremainegreen.co.uk

Terms from £188-£974 per week. Pets £18. **Tel: 01503 220333**

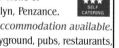

Nestling between farm and woodland, in an Area of Outstanding Natural Beauty lies Franchis, a quiet, friendly, 16-acre site, perfect for families looking for the type of old-fashioned holiday they enjoyed as children.

- Just minutes away from numerous sandy beaches, Flambards Theme Park and the Helford River; great for messing about on boats!
- 4 acres of fields contain 70 pitches, most with electric hook-up, and plenty of water points.
- No bars or entertainment but plenty of green space for your children to run around and play games in.
- Pitch prices start at just £10.
- We also have 5 chalets and 7 static caravans available for hire.

Visit our website or call for more details.
We look forward to hearing from you!

Franchis Holidays
**Near Mullion,
Cornwall TR12 7AZ
Tel 01326 240301
enquiries@franchis.co.uk
www.franchis.co.uk**

SOUTH DEVON

 ## Best Beaches

As Britain's prime holiday area it is not surprising that South Devon is rich in fine beaches. Quality Coast Awards went to several beaches around this delightful coastline, where standards of cleanliness, safety and environmental management satisfied strict criteria.

[i] South West Tourism
(Bristol & Bath, Cornwall, Devon, Dorset, Gloucestershire & The Cotswolds, Somerset, Wiltshire).

- Tel: 0870 442 0880
- Fax: 0870 442 0881
- e-mail: post@swtourism.co.uk
- www.visitsouthwest.co.uk

BLUE FLAG BEACHES 2007
- *Dawlish Warren*
- *Bantham*
- *Blackpool Sands*
- *Challaborough*
- *Bigbury-on-Sea*
- *Salcombe, South Sands*
- *Sandy Bay*
- *Torbay*
  Breakwater
  Goodrington Sands
  Meadfoot
  Oddicombe
  Broadsands

For more information about holidaying in South Devon see:
- www.visitsouthdevon.co.uk
- www.southdevonaonb.org.uk (Area of Outstanding Natural Beauty)
- www.englishriviera.co.uk

EXMOUTH

⚎ **Family Fun Activities:** Indoor swimming pool, children's playground, boating lake, indoor sports centre, amusement arcade, mini-railway • Bowls, tennis, indoor tennis centre, putting, cricket, approach golf • Boat trips, angling • Old tyme and modern dancing,

☆ **Special Events:** End July: Carnival events. October: Winter Floodlit Carnival.

ⓘ **Tourist Information Centre, Alexandra Terrace, Exmouth EX8 INZ 01395 222299 e-mail: info@exmouthtourism.co.uk www.exmouthguide.co.uk**

⛰ **Beaches**

• MAER, RODNEY BAY AND EXMOUTH BEACH. Beaches two-and-a-half miles long. Rodney Bay naturally sheltered, others open; promenade and good parking. *Safety and maintenance:* warning flags, lifeguards peak summer season; cleaned daily. *Beach facilities:* deck chairs, swings; beach huts for hire from T.I.C.; ice-cream kiosks, snack bars, restaurants and pubs; toilets with ♿ access. *Dog restrictions:* banned from main beach from 1st May to 30th September.

PLYMOUTH

⚎ **Family Fun Activities:** Plymouth Pavilions with leisure pool, ice-skating, bar, bistro and shops • Mayflower Visitor Centre • Plymouth Dome heritage centre • Crownhill Fort • National Marine Aquarium • Sports centre, indoor and outdoor swimming pools, parks with children's playgrounds • Tennis, putting, bowls, squash, dry-ski slope, bowling with quasar • Marina and water sports centre, sailing schools, sea angling • Theatre, multi-screen cinemas; museum and art gallery.

☆ **Special Events:** May: Lord Mayor's Day Procession; Half Marathon, Vehicle and Bus Rally. June: Plymouth Playfair. July: Saltram Fair. July: World Championship Powerboat Race. August: National Fireworks Championships. September: Heritage Open Days. November: Christmas Lights.

ⓘ **Tourist Information Centre, Plymouth Mayflower, The Barbican, Plymouth (01752 306330) e-mail: barbicantic@plymouth.gov.uk www.visitplymouth.co.uk**

⛰ **Beaches**

• BEACHES. The city itself has an attractive waterfront with sheltered promenades and rock pools, and a fully restored Art Deco Lido. There are good parking facilities, toilets, ice-cream kiosks, snack bars, and family restaurants/pubs.

SIDMOUTH

⚎ **Family Fun Activities:** Children's playgrounds • Cricket, golf, angling, sailing, putting, tennis, bowls.

☆ **Special Events:** August: International Folk Festival. September: Sidmouth Carnival.

ⓘ **Tourist Information Centre, Ham Lane, Sidmouth • 01395 516441 e-mail: enquiries@sidmouth.co.uk www.visitsidmouth.co.uk**

⛰ **Beaches**

• MAIN BEACH. Half-a-mile long, shingle and sand at low tide; promenade and ample parking. *Safety and maintenance:* lifeguards present only on Sundays; cleaned daily. *Beach facilities:* beach huts, deck chairs; ice-cream kiosk; toilets with ♿ access. *Dog restrictions:* banned from 1st May to 30th September.

TEIGNMOUTH & SHALDON

⚓ Family Fun Activities: Victorian Pier • Children's play area • Outdoor heated pool • Crazy golf • Bowls • Angling • Golf course • Summer shows.

☆ Special Events: **June:** Folk Festival. **July/August:** Summer Fun Fest. **July:** Carnival and Regatta. **August:** Water Carnival and Regatta. **November:** Jazz Festival, Winter Carnival.

ℹ Tourist Information Centre, The Den, Teignmouth TQ14 8BE • 01626 215666. e-mail: teigntic@teignbridge.gov.uk www.southdevon.org.uk

⛰ Beaches

• **TEIGNMOUTH TOWN BEACH.** Long, sandy beach stretching from mouth of River Teign east towards Dawlish. *Safety and maintenance:* information signage, lifeguard patrol May-Sept; lifesaving equipment; daily beach cleaning. *Beach facilities:* deck chairs; beach wheelchair for hire; ice-cream kiosks and snack bars; toilets, showers; (♿ access to beach). *Dog restrictions:* not allowed on designated areas of the beach from 1st May to 30th Sept.

• **NESS BEACH, SHALDON.** Shingle beach sloping gently to the sea; safe bathing, rock pools at low tide No ♿ access. *Safety and maintenance:* lifesaving equipment, information signage; daily beach cleaning. *Beach facilities:* shops and toilets nearby. *Dog restrictions:* none.

FREE AND REDUCED RATE HOLIDAY VISITS!
Don't miss our Readers' Offer Vouchers on pages 9-44

DAWLISH

⚓ Family Fun Activities: Sports centre •Amusement arcades • Approach golf, putting, crazy golf, bowls • Angling • Theatre • Boat trips •Visitor Centre at Dawlish Warren Nature Reserve.

☆ Special Events: **June:** Arts Festival. **July/August:** Summer Fun Fest. **August:** Carnival.

ℹ Tourist Information Centre, The Lawn, Dawlish EX7 9PW • 01626 215665 e-mail: dawtic@teignbridge.gov.uk www.southdevon.org.uk

⛰ Beaches

• **DAWLISH TOWN BEACH.** Mixture of sand and shingle, gently sloping to sea; safe family beach a short walk from town centre; poor ♿ access. *Safety and maintenance:* information signage, lifesaving equipment; cleaned daily. *Beach facilities:* deck chairs, ice-cream kiosks and snack bars; toilets with ♿ access. *Dog restrictions:* not allowed on designated areas of the beach from 1st May to 30th September.

• **CORYTON COVE.** Secluded, sandy beach within easy walking distance of town centre; ♿ access. *Safety and maintenance:* information signage, lifesaving equipment; cleaned daily. *Beach facilities:* beach hut hire, snack bar; toilets with ♿ access, showers. *Dog restrictions:* not allowed on designated areas of the beach from 1st May to 30th September.

• **DAWLISH WARREN.** Golden sands backed by sand dunes; easy access from main roads, good public transport links; ♿ access. *Safety and maintenance:* information signage, lifeguards May to September, lifesaving equipment; cleaned daily. *Beach facilities:* deck chairs; ice-cream kiosks and snack bars; toilets with ♿ access, showers. *Dog restrictions:* not allowed from slipway to groyne from 1st April to 30th September.

TORQUAY

Family Fun Activities: Water ski-ing, windsurfing, sailing, angling • Indoor pools • Crazy golf, putting, tennis, squash, ten-pin bowling • Cinema, theatres, nightclubs, casino • Riviera Leisure Centre, museum, Babbacombe Model Village, cliff railway, Living Coasts.

Special Events: August: Torbay Royal Regatta.

i **The Tourist Centre, Vaughan Parade, Torquay TQ2 5JG • 0906 6801268 – calls charged at 25p per minute www.englishriviera.co.uk**

Beaches

• TORRE ABBEY SANDS. 600 yards long, sandy and naturally sheltered; & easy access, ample parking nearby. *Safety and maintenance:* warning flags, lifesaving equipment, first-aid post. *Beach facilities:* deck chairs/sunbeds for hire; cafe/ refreshments; toilets nearby. *Dog restrictions:* dogs banned.

• ANSTEY'S COVE. 220 yards long, rock and shingle. Access steep in places. Parking 10 minutes' walk. *Safety and maintenance:* warning flags, lifesaving equipment. *Beach facilities:* deck chair/ sunbed/chalet hire; refreshments, beach shop; toilets nearby. *Dog restrictions:* dogs allowed.

• MEADFOOT BEACH. 350 yards long, pebble and sand; easy access and ample parking. *Safety and maintenance:* lifesaving equipment. *Beach facilities:* deck chair/ sunbed/chalet hire; cafe/refreshments; toilets with baby changing facilities. *Dog restrictions:* allowed (Kilmorlie end).

• ODDICOMBE BEACH. 400 yards long, sand and shingle; access via clifflift. Parking 15 minutes' walk. *Safety and maintenance:* warning flags, lifesaving equipment, first aid post. *Beach facilities:* deck chair/sunbed hire; beach cafe/refreshments, beach shop; toilets with & access and baby changing facilities. *Dog restrictions:* banned.

PAIGNTON

Family Fun Activities: Pier • Quay West water park and beach resort • Steam railway, amusement arcade, zoo, leisure centre with swimming pool • Boat trips, angling • Squash, badminton, tennis, putting, golf, go karting • Multiplex cinema, theatre.

Special Events: July: It's A Knockout, Torbay Carnival. **August:** Paignton Regatta, Children's Festival.

i **Paignton TIC, Esplanade Road, Paignton TQ4 6ED • 0906 6801268 – calls charged at 25p per minute www.englishriviera.co.uk**

Beaches

• BROADSANDS BEACH. Sandy beach, one-and-a-half miles long; easy access and ample parking. *Safety and maintenance:* warning flags, life-saving equipment, first aid post. *Beach facilities:* deck chair/ sunbed/chalet hire; refreshments, beach shop; toilets with & access. *Dog restrictions:* banned.

• GOODRINGTON SANDS. 1200 yards long, sandy; ample parking. *Safety and maintenance:* warning flags. *Beach facilities:* deck chair/sunbed hire; cafe/refreshments and restaurant, beach shop; toilets with & access. *Dog restrictions:* banned on South Sands, allowed on North Sands.

• PAIGNTON SANDS. Sandy with rock pools, 1200 yards long; promenade and pier with arcades. *Safety and maintenance:* warning flags, life-saving equipment, first aid post. *Beach facilities:* deck chair/sunbed hire; cafe/refreshments, restaurant, beach shop; toilets with & access. *Dog restrictions:* banned.

• PRESTON SANDS. 600 yards long, sandy and naturally sheltered. *Safety and maintenance:* warning flags, life-saving equipment. *Beach facilities:* deck chair/ sunbed/chalet hire; cafe/refreshments, beach shop; toilets (toilets with & access nearby). *Dog restrictions:* banned.

BRIXHAM

Family Fun Activities: Indoor and outdoor swimming pools • Tennis, squash, mini-golf, putting, leisure centre • Fishing trips/cruises, sailing • Berry Head Country Park • Golden Hind replica, museums, aquarium.

☆ **Special Events: May:** Heritage Festival. **June:** Brixham Trawler Race. **July:** Mardi Gras. **August:** Brixham Regatta.

i **Brixham T.I.C., Old Market House, The Quay, Brixham TQ5 8AW 0906 6801268 – calls charged at 25p per minute**) **www.englishriviera.co.uk**

Beaches

• BREAKWATER BEACH. Shingle beach, 100 yards long; easy access and ample parking; & access difficult. *Safety and maintenance:* warning flags, life-saving equipment. *Beach facilities:* deck chairs; cafe/refreshments and restaurant, beach shop; toilets. *Dog restrictions:* banned.

• SHOALSTONE BEACH. Shingle, with rock pools and sea water swimming pool; & access difficult. *Safety and maintenance:* warning flags, lifeguards, life-saving equipment. *Beach facilities:* deck chair/ sunbed hire; cafe; toilets with baby changing facilities. *Dog restrictions:* allowed.

• ST MARY'S BAY. Sand and shingle, parking 10 minutes' walk; & access difficult. *Safety and maintenance:* swimming safe with care. *Dog restrictions:* allowed.

Woodlands Leisure Park, Blackawton, Dartmouth.
See Readers' Offer Voucher

☆ Fun for all the Family ☆

◆ **Babbacombe Model Village (01803 315315).** Masterpiece of miniature landscaping - hundreds of models and figures. **www.babbacombemodelvillage.co.uk**

◆ **Bickleigh Castle, near Tiverton (01884 855363).** Medieval romantic home with armoury, thatched Jacobean wing, early Norman chapel, moat and gardens.

◆ **Dartmoor Wildlife Park, Sparkwell (01752 837645).** Over 100 animals ranging from tigers, bears and wolves to birds of prey and even guinea pigs.

◆ **Kent's Cavern Show Caves, Torquay (01803 215136).** Stalactite caves of great beauty. Guided tours to discover the magic of Britain's earliest known settlement. **www.kents-cavern.co.uk**

◆ **National Marine Aquarium, Plymouth (01752 600301).** New attraction where memorable sights include a wall of ocean 15 metres wide and a shark theatre in over 700,000 litres of water. **www.nationalaquarium.co.uk**

◆ **Pennywell Farm & Wildlife Centre, Buckfastleigh (01364 642023).** A unique Devon family day out with hands-on activities and crafts. Ponies and piglets, quad bikes and train rides - there's always something going on. **www.pennywellfarmcentre.co.uk**

◆ **Paignton Zoo (01803 697500).** Over 300 species in spacious landscaped enclosures. Miniature railway, restaurant, activity centre. **www.paigntonzoo.org.uk**

◆ **Paignton and Dartmouth Steam Railway (01803 555872).** Seven-mile trip along the spectacular Torbay coast; gift shop, buffet. **www.paignton-steamrailway.co.uk**

◆ **River Dart Country Park, Ashburton (01364 652511).** Country fun for everyone - children's adventure playgrounds, nature trails, picnic meadow. **www.dartmoor.co.uk**

◆ **Sorley Tunnel Adventure Park, Kingsbridge (01548 854078).** A great all-weather day out, including Adventure World, Alien Play Planet, Equestrian World, Farm World - something for everyone.

◆ **South Devon Railway, Buckfastleigh (0845 345 1420).** Excursion trips on steam trains; museum, picnic area and play area. **www.southdevonrailway.org**

◆ **Woodlands Leisure Park, Dartmouth (01803 712598).** Lots of family fun activities, indoor and outdoor, plus hundreds of animals and birds. **www.woodlands-leisure-park.co.uk**

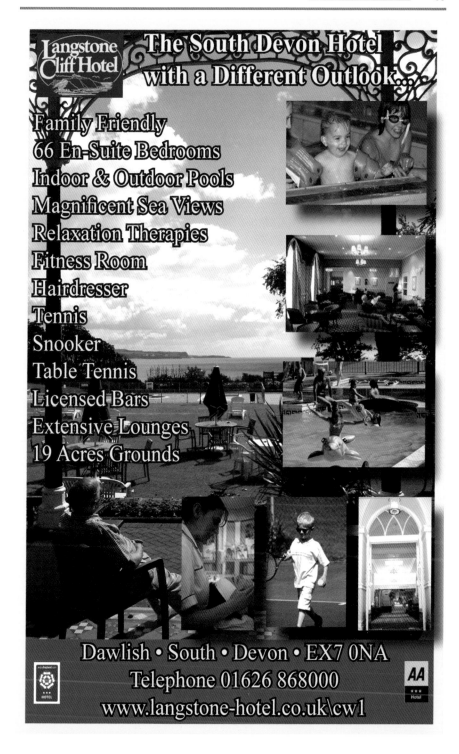

Come and stay on a real 400-acre farm in South Devon

Parkers Farm Cottages & Caravans

FARM COTTAGES
STATIC CARAVANS

Friendly, family-run self-catering complex with cottages and static caravans surrounded by beautiful countryside. 12 miles from the sea and close to Dartmoor National Park. Perfect for children and pets, with farm animals and plenty of space to roam. Large area to walk your dogs. Laundry, bar and restaurant. Good discounts for couples. A warm welcome awaits you.

How to find us from Exeter: Take A38 to Plymouth. When you see the sign "26 miles Plymouth", take the second left at Alston Cross signposted Woodland - Denbury. Continue past Parkers Farm Holiday Park, cottages on right hand side part way up hill

THE ROCKERY, CATON, ASHBURTON, DEVON TQ13 7LH

Tel: 01364 653008 • Fax: 01364 652915
parkerscottages@btconnect.com
www.parkersfarm.co.uk

★★★★
SELF
CATERING

NORTH DEVON

Best Beaches

Along with three other fine beaches from the area, Woolacombe Beach is once again a proud winner of a European Blue Flag, indicating strict beach management and the highest standard of bathing water under EC legislation. Quality Coast Awards also went to beaches in this area.

BLUE FLAG BEACHES 2007
- *Ilfracombe (Tunnels)*
- *Westward Ho!*
- *Woolacombe*
- *Croyde Bay*

[*i*] South West Tourism
(Bristol & Bath, Cornwall, Devon, Dorset, Gloucestershire & The Cotswolds, Somerset, Wiltshire).
- Tel: 0870 442 0880
- Fax: 0870 442 0881
- e-mail: post@swtourism.co.uk
- www.visitsouthwest.co.uk

FREE AND REDUCED RATE HOLIDAY VISITS!
Don't miss our Readers' Offer Vouchers on pages 9-44

For more information about holidaying in North Devon see:
- www.northdevon.com
- www.northdevon-aonb.org.uk (Area of Outstanding Natural Beauty)
- www.visit-exmoor.co.uk

LYNTON & LYNMOUTH

⌂ Family Fun Activities: Children's playgrounds • Putting, tennis, bowls, cricket, horse riding • Boat trips, river and sea fishing • Cinema • Brass rubbing, museum • Local crafts centre • Unique water-operated cliff railway linking twin resorts.

ⓘ **Tourist Information Centre, Town Hall, Lynton**
0845 660 3232 • Fax: 01598 752755
e-mail: info@lyntourism.co.uk
www.lyntourism.co.uk

🏖 Beaches

• LEE BAY BEACH. Half-a-mile long, sand and shingle, with access through Valley of Rocks and on to Lee Abbey bottom lodge (toll charge); parking in field overlooking sea. *Safety and maintenance:* safe within the bay, cleaned whenever necessary. *Beach facilities:* refreshments five minutes' walk (restricted opening), toilets two minutes' walk. *Dog restrictions:* banned.

• LYNMOUTH BEACH. Large rocky beach, long slipway, Rhenish tower guarding harbour. *Safety and maintenance:* safe within the bay, cleaned whenever necessary. *Dog restrictions:* none .

ILFRACOMBE

⌂ Family Fun Activities: Heated indoor pool, children's playground, boating lake, go karting, sports canoes • Pier, angling • Tennis, putting, pitch and putt, crazy golf, golf course • Theatre with shows all year round, cinema, discos.

ⓘ **Tourist Information Centre, The Promenade, Ilfracombe • 01271 863001 e-mail: info@ilfracombe-tourism.co.uk www.ilfracombe-tourism.co.uk**

☆ **Special Events:** **June:** Victorian Celebration. **July:** North Devon Arts Youth Festival. **August:** Emergency Rescue Service Display. **August/September:** Flower Shows.

🏖 Beaches

• HARBOUR BEACH. 200 yards long, sandy and naturally sheltered; good parking. Promenade, pier with arcade and cafe; toilets and parking. *Beach facilities:* ice-cream kiosks, snack bars, restaurants and pubs; toilets with ♿ access.

• HELE BAY BEACH. Half-a-mile long, shingle (some sand) with rock pools; promenade, good parking. *Safety and maintenance:* cleaned regularly during season. *Beach facilities:* deck chairs, sports canoes; ice-cream kiosk, snack bars, restaurants and pubs; toilets with ♿ access

• LARKSTONE BEACH. 100 yards long, shingle and rock pools, naturally sheltered; good parking. *Safety and maintenance:* cleaned regularly in season. *Beach facilities:* ice-cream kiosk; toilets with ♿ access.

• RAPPAREE BEACH. 220 yards long, shingle with rock pools and cliffs, naturally sheltered; promenade, good parking. *Safety and maintenance:* warning signs; certain parts cut off at high tide; cleaned regularly during season.

• TUNNELS BEACHES. 600 yards long, shingle with rock pools and cliffs; naturally sheltered, good parking. *Safety and maintenance:* warning signs, certain parts cut off at high tide; beach privately owned and cleaned daily during season. *Beach facilities:* deck chairs, sports canoes, rowing boats; ice-cream kiosk and snack bar; toilets.

• WHITE PEBBLE BEACH. 220 yards long, shingle and pebbles. Cliffs, naturally sheltered; parking. *Safety and maintenance:* warning signs, certain parts cut off at high tide.

• WILDERSMOUTH BEACH. 220 yards long, shingle with rock pools; naturally sheltered; promenade, good parking. *Safety and maintenance:* cleaned by Local Authority. *Beach facilities:* deck chairs; ice-cream kiosks, snack bars, restaurants and pubs; ramps with & access.

FHG Guides

publish a large range of well-known accommodation guides. We will be happy to send you details or you can use the order form at the back of this book.

WOOLACOMBE

Family Fun Activities: Repertory theatre and other entertainment in season.

☆ **Special Events: July:** Grand Sandcastle Competition. **September:** National Surf Life Saving Championships (every 3rd year). Other surf and water competitions during year.

[i] Tourist Information Centre, The Esplanade, Woolacombe EX34 7DL • 01271 870553 e-mail: woolacombetic@visit.org.uk www.woolacombetourism.co.uk

Beaches

WOOLACOMBE SANDS BEACH. 3 miles long, sandy and naturally sheltered; good parking. *Safety and maintenance:* flagged, warning signs, lifeguards (May to September); cleaned daily. *Beach facilities* (May to September): deck chairs, beach huts, children's amusements, ice-cream kiosks, snack bars, restaurants and pubs; toilets with & access. *Dog restrictions:* some restricted areas in operation May to September. Blue Flag and Seaside Award since 1991. England for Excellence Award for Best Family Holiday 1999.

Devon is a popular centre for walking and sailing

☆ Fun for all the Family ☆

◈ **Arlington Court (NT), Barnstaple (01271 850296).** A fascinating collection including shells and model ships. Surrounding park has Shetland ponies and a flock of Jacob's sheep. Teas and snacks.

◈ **The Big Sheep, Abbotsham (01237 472366).** All you ever wanted to know about sheep – lots of lambs, plus sheep dairy, shearing, sheepdog trials. Ewetopia indoor playground. Shop and restaurant. www.thebigsheep.co.uk

◈ **Gnome Reserve, Near Bradworthy (01409 241435).** For the young at heart - from 1 to 101! Four acres of woodland, meadow and garden is home to over 1000 gnomes and pixies. Gnome hats loaned free of charge to make you feel at home! www.gnomereserve.co.uk

◈ **Combe Martin Wildlife and Dinosaur Park (01271 882486).** Otters, falcons, nature walks, children's playground and zoo, large indoor model railway. www.dinosaur-park.com

◈ **Dartington Crystal, Torrington (01805 626244).** Marvel at the glass-blower's skill and trace the development of manufacturing techniques over the centuries. Factory shop and restaurant. www.dartington.co.uk

◈ **Escot Park, Ottery St Mary (01404 822188).** Enjoy the gardens and fantasy woodland which surround this historic house. Maze, aquatic and pet centre, craft and gift shop - a place fop people who love Nature. www.escot-devon.co.uk

◈ **Exmoor Zoological Park, Bratton Fleming (01598 763352).** Formal and natural gardens with a large collection of tropical birds. Tarzanland for children; tearoom and gift shop. www.exmoorzoo.co.uk

◈ **Jungleland, Barnstaple (01271 343884).** Collection of plants from all over the world in near as possible natural settings.

◈ **The Milky Way, Clovelly (01237 431255).** Hand milk a cow, bottle feed lambs, goats and calves. Adventure playground and old farm machinery. www.themilkyway.co.uk

◈ **Once Upon A Time, Woolacombe (01271 870900).** Children's park with train rides, adventure trails, soft play area.

◈ **Rosemoor Garden, Great Torrington (01805 624067).** Garden (now RHS) started in 1959: rhododendrons, ornamental trees and shrubs, primulas, young arboretum. www.rhs.org.uk/gardens/rosemoor

See the **Family-Friendly Pubs & Inns**
Supplement on pages 177-180 for establishments
which really welcome children

CHILDREN • FREE ACCOMMODATION

ETC ★★★

Sandy Cove Hotel stands in 20 acres of cliff, coast and garden. The Hotel Restaurant overlooks the sea and cliffs with spectacular views of the bay. Mini-breaks are available as well as special weekly rates, all of which offer a five-course meal including seafood platters with lobster, smoked salmon and steak. Every Saturday there is a Swedish Smorgasbord and Carvery followed by dancing till late. All bedrooms have colour TV, telephone, teamaking and are en suite. There is an unique indoor swimming pool with rolling back sides to enjoy the sun, as well as a whirlpool, sauna, steam-room and fitness area with gym equipment.

Please return this advertisement to qualify for "Pets Stay Free" offer.
Children have free accommodation sharing parents' room.
Children under 5 years completely free, including meals.

You'll love the special atmosphere of Sandy Cove, why not find us on our website at
www.sandycove-hotel.co.uk or ring to request a brochure

SANDY COVE
HOTEL

Combe Martin Bay,
Devon EX34 9SR
Tel: 01271 882243
     01271 882888

Looking for holiday accommodation?
search for details of properties where children are welcome
www.holidayguides.com

SOMERSET & WILTSHIRE

 **Best Beaches**

There are some fine beaches in this delightful part of the country, including some of the West Country's most popular family holiday resorts. A Quality Coast Award has been gained in 2007 by Burnham-on-Sea.

 South West Tourism
(Bristol & Bath, Cornwall, Devon, Dorset, Gloucestershire & The Cotswolds, Somerset, Wiltshire).

* Tel: 0870 442 0880
* Fax: 0870 442 0881
* e-mail: post@swtourism.co.uk
* www.visitsouthwest.co.ukv

FHG Guides

publish a large range of well-known accommodation guides.
We will be happy to send you details or you can use
the order form at the back of this book.

For more information about holidaying in Somerset see:

• www.visitsomerset.co.uk

• www.somersetcoast.com

For more information about holidaying in Wiltshire see:

• www.visitwiltshire.co.uk

MINEHEAD

Family Fun Activities: New look seafront with extensive sandy beach • Aquasplash Leisure Pool with wave machine • cruises and steam train rides • Horse riding and walking on nearby Exmoor • Theatre • Classic Car Collection • Butlins Family Entertainment Resort with a host of attractions including funfair, go karts, cinema, leisure pool and live shows.

☆ **Special Events:** Late April/early May: Hobby Horse festivities. **July:** Minehead and Exmoor Festival; Friends of Thomas the Tank Engine Weekend.

i Tourist Information Centre, **17 Friday Street, Minehead TA24 5UB 01643 702624 • Fax: 01643 707166 e-mail: mineheadtic@visit.org.uk www.minehead.co.uk**

Beaches

• MINEHEAD STRAND BEACH. Wide sandy beach with access down ramps from new sea wall. Ample parking. *Safety and maintenance:* cleaned daily. *Beach facilities:* cafe and takeaway food outlets; toilets with ♿ access. *Dog restrictions:* not allowed on beach from 1st May to 30th September; must be kept on lead on promenade.

• MINEHEAD TERMINUS BEACH. A mixture of sand and pebbles (continuation of the Strand in a westwards direction). *Facilities and Dog Restrictions:* as for Strand beach.

WESTON-SUPER-MARE

Family Fun Activities: The SeaQuarium • Grand Pier with amusements, land train, miniature railway, kids' play area • Marine lake • Donkey rides, amusements •Leisure centre • Tennis, putting, bowls, pitch and putt, ten-pin bowling, riding, rugby, football, cricket, fishing, golf • Cinema, museum, shows, night clubs, live music.

☆ **Special Events:** for a full up-to-date listing of events visit **www.somersetcoast.com** or call the Tourist Information Centre. Events include national waterski races, Holidays, children's activities, Playhouse shows, motorcycle beach race and carnival.

i Tourist Information Centre, **Beach Lawns, Weston-super-Mare BS23 1AT 01934 888800 Minicom: 01934 643172 westontouristinfo@n-somerset.gov.uk www.somersetcoast.com**

Beaches

• BEACH. Two miles long, sandy with rock pools and shingle at Anchor Head. Promenade and piers; good parking. *Safety and maintenance:* beach cleaned daily all year. *Beach facilities:* deck chairs, donkeys and pony carts, marine lake and fun castle; ice-cream kiosks, snack bars, restaurants and pubs; toilets, some with ♿ access. *Dog restrictions:* dog ban on section of main beach between May and September.

☆ Fun for all the Family ☆

◆ **Avon Valley Railway, near Bristol (0117 932 5538).** Working railway museum with locos and coaches. Enjoy a 5-mile trip along the lovely River Avon valley.
www.avonvalleyrailway.co.uk

◆ **Bee World and Animal Centre, Stogumber (01984 656545).** Unravel the mysteries of bee-keeping and meet lots of friendly animals at this unique "hands-on" centre. Children's play area.

◆ **Bristol Zoo (0117 974 7300).** Extensive and fascinating collection including pygmy hippos and gorillas. Over 300 species from lions to dung beetles.
www.bristolzoo.org.uk

◆ **Cheddar Caves & Gorge (01934 742343).** Famous for its caves and underground pools, in a deep winding fissure in the Mendip Hills. Exhibitions.
www.chedddarcaves.co.uk

◆ **Cholderton Rare Breeds Farm Park, near Salisbury** (01980 629438). Rare and endangered breeds of British farm animals, plus Rabbit World with over 50 varieties. Pig racing (Pork Stakes) in peak season.
www.choldertoncharliesfarm.com

◆ **Cricket St Thomas Wildlife Park, near Chard (01460 30111).** Large collection of wild animals and birds in 1000 acres of woodland and lakes.
www.cstwp.co.uk

◆ **Haynes Motor Museum, Sparkford, Near Yeovil (01963 440804).** Magnificent collection of over 250 vintage, veteran and classic cars, and 50 motorcycles. Experience 100 smiles per hour!
www.haynesmotormuseum.co.uk

◆ **Longleat Safari Park, Warminster (01985 844400).** 100-acre reserve for lions, giraffes, monkeys, zebras and tigers roaming free. World's longest hedge maze, Postman Pat village.
www.longleat.co.uk

◆ **Rode Bird Gardens, near Bath (01373 830326).** 17 acres of beautifully laid out grounds with hundreds of exquisitely coloured birds. Children's play area.

◆ **SS Great Britain, Bristol (0117 926 0680).** Splendid six-masted ocean going vessel dating from 1843 and associated with engineering genius Isambard Kingdom Brunel.
www.ss-great-britain.com

◆ **SeaQuarium, Weston-super-Mare (01934 613361).** Exciting close encounters with marvels of marine life, from starfish to sharks. Feeding demonstrations, talks and special presentations.
www,seaquarium.co.uk

◆ **STEAM - Museum of Great Western Railway, Swindon (01793 466646).** Fun hands-on exhibits and rare archive footage tell the story of this famous railway company.
www.steam-museum.org.uk

◆ **West Somerset Railway, Bishops Lydeard (01643 704996).** A nostalgic journey through the unspoilt beauty of the Quantock Hills and along the coast; Visitor Centre and model railway.
www.west-somerset-railway.co.uk

◆ **Wookey Hole, Wells (01749 672243).** Britain's most spectacular caves, with dramatic lighting effects. Also paper making demonstrations, Magical Mirror Maze.
www.wookey.co.uk

HAMPSHIRE & DORSET

 Best Beaches

No less than 11 beaches in the area have won European Blue Flag Awards for 2007, and a Quality Coast Award has been gained by Swanage Central.

BLUE FLAG BEACHES 2007

- *Bournemouth*
  - *Fisherman's Walk*
  - *Alum Chine*
  - *Durley Chine*
  - *Southbourne*
- *Poole*
  - *Canford Cliffs Chine*
  - *Sandbanks*
  - *Shore Road*
  - *Branksome Chine*
- *Swanage Central*
- *West Beachlands Central*
- *West Beachlands West*

[i] South East England Tourism
- Tel: 023 8062 5400
- Fax: 023 8062 0010
- e-mail: enquiries@tourismse.com
- www.visitsoutheastengland.com

[i] South West Tourism
(Bristol & Bath, Cornwall, Devon, Dorset, Gloucs & The Cotswolds, Somerset, Wiltshire).
- Tel: 0870 442 0880
- Fax: 0870 442 0881
- e-mail: post@swtourism.co.uk
- www.visitsouthwest.co.uk

For more information about holidaying in Dorset see:
- www.dorsetforyou.com
- www.westdorset.com (West Dorset)
- www.ruraldorset.com (North Dorset)
- www.dorset-newforest.com

For more information about holidaying in Hampshire see:
- www.vist-hampshire.co.uk

BOURNEMOUTH

⛱ **Family Fun Activities:** Seven miles of golden sand, first-class attractions, beautiful gardens and summer festivals offer something for everyone from the Oceanarium to the Bournemouth International Centre and the Russell-Cotes Museum. There is plenty to do whatever the weather. Try the Bournemouth Eye tethered balloon ride.
Free 'Family Fun' brochure available on request from Visitor Information Bureau.

☆ **Special Events:** **School Summer Holidays:** Kids Fun Festival with more than 100 free shows and activities. Sporting events, competitions and festivals take place throughout the year.

ℹ **Visitor Information Bureau, Westover Road, Bournemouth BH1 2BU** Information line and accommodation enquiries: 0845 0511700
e-mail: info@bournemouth.gov.uk
www.bournemouth.co.uk

🏖 Beaches

• BEACH. 7 miles long, sandy with traffic-free promenade, reached by zig-zag paths or cliff lifts. *Safety and maintenance:* lifeguard patrols, close-circuit TV surveillance, first-aid posts; cleaned twice daily. *Beach facilities:* children's beach GameZone in summer; rowing boats, pedalos, speed boats, kayaks, surfing; beach hut hire. "No Smoking" zones. Special 'Kidzone' safety areas. Excellent catering facilities. *Dog restrictions:* Dog-friendly sections of beach at Fisherman's Walk and Alum Chine between May and September inclusive; allowed on the promenade on lead.

POOLE

⛱ **Family Fun Activities:** Poole Quay with shops, crafts, museums, Poole pottery, restaurants • Crab lining, fishing trips, harbour boat trips, wind-surfing and sailing in Europe's largest natural harbour • Brownsea Island and road train • Poole Park with Gus Gorilla's indoor playground, crazy golf, Poole Park train, mini icerink • Sports centres with swimming, badminton, squash, etc • Tower Park Entertainment Centre with cinema, Bowlplex, Splashdown, restaurants • Monkey World • Poole Museum with free entry.
Free 'Family Fun' brochure available on request from Poole Tourist Office.

☆ **Special Events:** **May/September:** programme of spectacular weekday events featuring motorcycles, car nostalgia, fireworks, speedway, live entertainment, children's activities. **September:** Animal Windfest.

ℹ **Poole Welcome Centre, Enefco House, Poole Quay, Poole BH15 1HJ**
01202 253253
e-mail: tourism@pooletourism.com
www.pooletourism.com

🏖 Beaches

• BEACH. Three miles of sands stretching from Sandbanks to Branksome Dene Chine. 7 car parks. *Safety and maintenance:* cleaned daily; lifeguard coverage in main season, beach station at Sandbanks manned throughout year. *Beach facilities:* beach huts, deckchairs and windbreaks for hire; watersports; ice-cream kiosks, snacks and cafe; toilets with ♿ facilities. *Dog restrictions:* banned from main beaches from May to September, must be kept on lead on promenade at all times.

A useful index of towns/counties appears on page 181

SWANAGE

Family Fun Activities: Bowling green, tennis, putting, crazy golf, 18-hole pitch and putt course, trampolines • Swanage Bay View Restaurant • Holiday park with swimming pool, skittle alley, indoor bowls and trimnasium • Water ski-ing, windsurfing, sailing, motor boats, sea angling • Castle, lighthouse, country park • Theatre/cinema.

Special Events: **July:** Swanage Jazz Festival. **August:** Regatta and Carnival Week. **September:** Swanage Folk Festival

i **Tourist Information Centre, Shore Road, Swanage BH19 1LB** • **0870 4420680** **e-mail: mail@swanage.gov.uk** **www.swanage.gov.uk**

Beaches

• SWANAGE BAY BEACH. Three miles long, sandy and naturally sheltered; promenade and good parking. *Safety and maintenance:* cleaned daily. *Beach facilities:* deck chairs, Punch and Judy; pedalcraft; toilets with & facilities. *Dog restrictions:* banned from main beach from 1st May to 30th September; must be kept on lead on promenade.

WEYMOUTH

Family Fun Activities: Country Park with Model World, Sea Life Park, Miniature Railway, Mini-Golf, Leisure Ranch and RSPB Nature Reserve • Weymouth Old Harbour including Brewers Quay Complex and Weymouth Timewalk, Deep Sea Adventure, Nothe Fort and Gardens, Tudor House. • Pleasure cruises, float and boat hire, sailing, sub-aqua sports • Tennis, bowls • Swimming pool • Theatre with family shows, cinemas, night clubs • Superbowl

Special Events: **May:** Beach Kite Festival, Trawler Race and Water Carnival. **July/August:** Beach Volleyball Championships. **August:** weekly Firework Festival, Weymouth Carnival. **October:** Beach Motocross.

i **Tourist Information, King's Statue, Weymouth** • **01305 785747** **e-mail: tourism@weymouth.gov.uk** **www.visitweymouth.co.uk**

Beaches

• WEYMOUTH BAY BEACH. Two and a half miles long, sand running into shingle; promenade and piers. *Safety and maintenance:* Beach Control Centre, lifeguards; first aid and lost children post; beach cleaned daily. *Beach facilities:* deck chairs, Punch and Judy, trampolines, amusement arcades; floats, canoes; ice-cream kiosks, restaurants and pubs; toilets with & facilities. *Dog restrictions:* dogs restricted to special areas May-September.

Poole Quay, Dorset

☆ Fun for all the Family ☆

◆ **Adventure Wonderland, Christchurch (01202 483444).** Guaranteed fun whatever the weather for 2-12 year olds. Also Wild Thing indoor play centre with themed and interactive equipment, and Alice Maze.
www.adventurewonderland.co.uk

◆ **Beaulieu (01590 612345).** National Motor Museum – motoring heritage brought back to life. Includes James Bond Experience. Also 13th century Abbey and Monastic Life exhibition.
www.beaulieu.co.uk

◆ **Blue Reef Aquarium, Portsmouth (02392 875222).** Innovative displays provide an insight into the mysterious world of the deep. Restaurant and children's attractions.
www.bluereefaquarium.co.uk

◆ **Dinosaur Museum, Dorchester (01305 269741).** Children of all ages love these scaly creatures, so make for this superb "hands on" exhibition dedicated entirely to dinosaurs.
www.thedinosaurmuseum.com

◆ **Longdown Activity Farm, Ashurst, Near Southampton** (023 8029 2837). Lots of hands-on activities every day, including small animal handling sessions, plus indoor and outdoor play areas. Gift shop and tearoom.
www.longdownfarm.co.uk

◆ **Marwell Zoological Park, near Winchester (01962 777407).** 200-acre park with rare wild animals including tigers, zebras, cheetahs, leopards, etc. Children's zoo, picnic area, cafe.
www.marwell.org.uk

◆ **New Forest Museum and Visitor Centre, Lyndhurst (023 8028 3444).** Learn the story of the Forest in an audio-visual show; gift shop specialising in local crafts.
www.newforestmuseum.org.uk

◆ **Paultons Park, near Romsey (023 8081 4442).** A fun-filled day out at this family leisure park with rides and thrills galore. Over 40 attractions/rides.
www.paultonspark.co.uk

◆ **Tank Museum, Bovington, near Wareham (01929 405096).** Tanks and armoured cars from all over the world; "drive a tank" simulator; gift shop and restaurant.
www.tankmuseum.co.uk

◆ **Teddy Bear Museum, Dorchester (01305 266040).** From the earliest antique teddy bears to today's TV favourites, they are all waiting to greet you. Collectors' shop, House with family of human-size bears.
www.teddybearhouse.co.uk

See the **Family-Friendly Pubs & Inns**
Supplement on pages 177-180 for establishments
which really welcome children

ISLE OF WIGHT

🏖 Best Beaches 🏖

The varied coastline of the Isle of Wight includes many safe, sandy beaches. Colwell, Cowes, East Cowes and Gurnard have won a Quality Coast Award, and three beaches have earned the right to fly a Blue Flag.

BLUE FLAG BEACHES 2007
- *Ryde East*
- *Shanklin*
- *Sandown*

 Isle of Wight Tourism
- Tel: 01983 813813
- Fax: 01983 823031
- e-mail: info@islandbreaks.co.uk
- www.islandbreaks.co.uk

Ryde, Sea View & St Helens

🏖 **Family Fun Activities:** Boating lake, bowling alley, swimming pool, ice skating rink, cinema • Dotto train along seafront and into town • Flamingo Park where children can hand-feed penguins, macaws and parrots • Travel back in time on the Isle of Wight steam railway.

☆ **Special Events: July:** Ryde Regatta. **August/September:** Ryde Carnival.

🏖 **Beaches**

• BEACH. Coastline three-and-a-half miles long; sand at Ryde, rockpools at Seaview; ample parking. *Safety and maintenance:* inshore rescue; cleaned daily. *Beach facilities:* canoe lake on esplanade, swimming pools, playground, mini fun fair, trampolines; snack bars and restaurants (some licensed); toilets with ♿ access. *Dog restrictions:* banned on main areas of beach from 1st May to 30th September; must be kept on lead on promenade; "poop scoop" regulations in force.

Sandown & Lake

🏖 **Family Fun Activities:** Fishing, tennis, basketball, putting, pitch and putt, crazy golf
- Pier with bowling and other attractions
- Street market • Zoo • Leisure centre
- Dinosaur Isle • Dotto train • Go-karts.

☆**Special Events:** July/August: Carnival. **August:** Regatta. **October:** White Air Extreme Sports Festival.

Beaches

• BEACH. Approximately three miles long, sandy with cliffs at back; promenade, pier complex with bar, restaurant, amusements and boat trips. *Safety and maintenance:* warning flags, lifeguards; cleaned daily in season. Kidzone in selected parts. *Beach facilities:* deck chairs, windsurfing, pedalcraft, children's entertainment; snack bars on promenade open during summer season; toilets with ♿ access. *Dog restrictions:* banned from main areas of beach from 1st May to 30th September; "poop scoop"regulations in force.

Ventnor

Family Fun Activities: Botanic Gardens and Winter Gardens with regular entertainment • Golf • Paddling pool • Marina • Nearby Blackgang Chine has attractions and rides for the whole family.

☆ **Special Events:** **April:** Jazz Divas. **August:** Carnival.

Beaches

• BEACH. Approximately quarter-of-a-mile long; mainly sand, some shingle; promenade. *Safety and maintenance:* cleaned daily. *Beach facilities:* deck chairs; snack bars and restaurants, amusements; public house; toilets with ♿ access. *Dog restrictions:* banned on main beach areas from 1st May to 30th September; "poop scoop" regulations in force.

Colwell & Totland

Small resort on Totland Bay, three miles south-west of Yarmouth.

Beaches

• BEACH. One-and-a-half miles long; sandy at Colwell, sand with some shingle at Totland; sea wall connects the two bays. *Safety and maintenance:* partly cleaned daily in season. *Beach facilities:* deck chairs and paddlecraft at Colwell; snacks and ice-cream at both locations. *Dog restrictions:* not allowed on Colwell beach between 1st May and 30th September.

Shanklin

Family Fun Activities: Water activities • Indoor play area, crazy golf, golf, putting • Dotto train • Cliff lift to town.

☆ **Special Events:** Shanklin Theatre shows. **August:** Shanklin Town regatta and sea events.

Beaches

• BEACH. Sandy beach, access via cliff lift; two-mile long promenade connects town to Sandown. Shanklin Chine illuminated on summer evenings. *Beach facilities:* refreshments, toilets; deck chairs, beach huts. *Dog restrictions:* banned from main beach from 1st May to 30th September.

Yarmouth

One of the oldest towns on the Island with a busy harbour. Boat trips to Needles from pier. Nearby attractions include Fort Victoria, Dimbola Lodge and Dinosaur Farm Museum.

☆ **Special Events:** **June:** Old Gaffers Festival.

Beaches

• BEACH. Shingle beach with pier; swimming at Sandhard area. *Beach facilities:* refreshments; toilets . *Dog restrictions:* must be kept on lead.

☆ Fun for all the Family ☆

◆ **Amazon World, Newchurch (01983 867122).** All-weather Amazon Rain Forest attraction with over 200 species of birds and animals. Falconry displays.
www.amazonworld.co.uk

◆ **Blackgang Chine, Chale (01983 730052).** 40 acres of cliff top gardens, exhibitions, fantasy attractions – Cowboy Town, Nurseryland, Giant Snakes 'n' Ladders, Water Force, a 100m high speed boat ride.
www.blackgangchine.com

◆ **Brickfields Horse Country, near Ryde (01983 566801).** From mighty Shires to miniature Shetland ponies. Unique collections of bygones, children's farm corner, restaurant and bar.
www.brickfields.net

◆ **Butterfly World and Fountain World, Wootton (01983 883430).** Hundreds of exotic butterflies and insects; displays of fountains and indoor gardens. Play area.

◆ **Dinosaur Isle, Sandown (01983 404344).** Exciting new exhibition centre in a spectacular pterosaur-shaped building, with life-size dinosaurs; guided fossil walks to sites of interest on the island.
www.dinosaurisle.com

◆ **Isle of Wight Steam Railway, Near Ryde (01983 882204).** 5½ mile round trip on genuine vintage train. Station at Havenstreet with museum, shop, cafe and bar.
www.iwsteamrailway.co.uk

◆ **Isle of Wight Wax Works, Brading (01983 407286/0870 4584477).** World-famous museum set in 11th century rectory mansion. Visit the Chamber of Horrors and Animal World.

◆ **Isle of Wight Zoo, Sandown (01983 405562).** Big cats, snakes and spiders. Cafe, play areas, animal contact area — be photographed with a snake!
www.isleofwightzoo.com

◆ **Natural History Centre, Godshill (01983 840333).** A fascinating display of tropical seashells, birds, butterflies and even a lizard embalmed in amber, all housed in a 17th century coach house.
www.shellmuseum.co.uk

◆ **Needles Park, Alum Bay (0870 458 0022).** A great family day out with attractions including chairlift, dare-devil rides, crazy golf, glass-making studio, sweet making; restaurant.
www.theneedles.co.uk

◆ **Osborne House, East Cowes (01983 200022).** Magnificent residence much loved by Queen Victoria. The 'Swiss Cottage' in the grounds was the playroom of the royal children; carriage rides through the grounds.

◆ **Robin Hill Country Park, near Newport (01983 527352).** Activities for all ages: Time Machine and Colossus rides; Countryside Centre, Play Village, Splash Attack and lots more.
www.robin-hill.com

◆ **Shipwreck Centre and Maritime Museum, Bembridge (01983 872223/ 873125).** Museum devoted to local maritime heritage. Shipwreck artefacts, ship models, diving equipment etc.

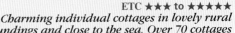

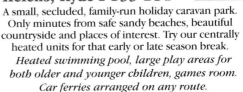

FHG Guides

publish a large range of well-known accommodation guides.
We will be happy to send you details or you can use
the order form at the back of this book.

SUSSEX

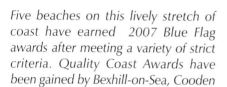

Five beaches on this lively stretch of coast have earned 2007 Blue Flag awards after meeting a variety of strict criteria. Quality Coast Awards have been gained by Bexhill-on-Sea, Cooden Beach, and Eastbourne.

[i] South East England Tourism
• Tel: 023 8062 5400
• Fax: 023 8062 0010
• e-mail: enquiries@tourismse.com
• www.visitsoutheastengland.com

BLUE FLAG BEACHES 2007
• **West Wittering**
• **Eastbourne (Pier to Wish Tower)**
• **Bognor Regis (East)**
• **Hove Lawns**
• **West Street**

For more information about holidaying in Sussex see:
• www.visitsussex.org
• www.sussexbythesea.com
• www.eastsussex.gov.uk

BRIGHTON

⚓ Family Fun Activities: Brighton Pier, Sea Life Centre, Royal Pavilion, Brighton Museum, British Engineerium, Preston Manor, Foredown Tower, West Blatchington Windmill, Fishing Museum, National Museum of Penny Slot Machines; Marina Village • Fishing, boat trips, windsurfing, sailing • Horse racing, greyhound racing • 10-pin bowling, putting, crazy golf, pitch and putt, golf courses, skate boarding, roller blading, ice skating, tennis, squash, bowls, badminton, cycle hire, indoor swimming pools • Cinemas, theatres, nightclubs, discos • Churchill Square, North Laine and Lanes shopping districts with family-friendly restaurants and cafes.

☆ Special Events: May: Brighton Festival. June: London-Brighton Bike Ride. July: Kite Festival. August: Circus. November: Veteran Car Run.

ℹ️ VisiitBrighton, Royal Pavilion Shop, 4-5 Pavilion Buildings, Brighton BNI IEE 0906 711 2255 brighton-tourism@brighton-hove.gov.uk www.visitbrighton.com

🏖 Beaches

• BEACH. 7 miles long, shingle and rockpools; cliff walk, promenade with Volks Railway, pier with funfair and arcades. Artists' and fishing quarters. Naturist area at eastern end of promenade, near marina; warning flags, lifeguards (some undertow at extreme eastern end); cleaned daily in season. *Beach facilities:* deck chairs; ramp and lift to lower promenade; paddling pool, new children's play area; volleyball; basketball; showers; ice-cream kiosks, snack bars, restaurants and pubs; toilets with & access, baby changing facilities. *Dog restrictions:* dogs allowed from West Pier to Hove boundary and from Volks Railway to Banjo Groyne. Not allowed on any other part of the beach.

BOGNOR REGIS

⚓ Family Fun Activities: Free summer Sunday afternoon bandstand concerts in Hotham Park • Playgrounds, amusement arcades, tennis, putting, crazy golf, golf course, sailing • Cinema • Day visitors welcome at Butlins Family Entertainment Centre • Miniature railway in Hotham Park.

☆ Special Events: Various events throughout the summer including: Bognor Birdman (the original), Sands of Time Seaside Festival, Illumination Gala and Procession, Here Comes Summer.

ℹ️ Visitor Information Centre, Belmont Street, Bognor Regis • 01243 823140 e-mail: bognorregis.vic@arun.gov.uk www.sussexbythesea.com

🏖 Beaches

• BEACH. 8 miles long, sand and shingle, naturally sheltered; promenade and pier with arcades; ample voucher parking. *Safety and maintenance:* warning signs, rocks at low tide; cleaned regularly. *Beach facilities:* deck chairs, showers, children's play area; Kidcare Scheme along 50-metre stretch of seafront; seafront landtrain; ice-cream kiosks, snack bars, restaurants, pubs; toilets (toilets with & access on sea front). *Dog restrictions:* not allowed on main beach from May to September.

EASTBOURNE

⛭ **Family Fun Activities:** Fort Fun and Treasure Island theme parks, Miniature Steam Railway, Sovereign Centre, Knockhatch Adventure Park, Drusillas Zoo, Seven Sisters Sheep Centre, Museum of Shops, Redoubt Fortress, Lifeboat Museum, historic Pevensey Castle and Michelham Priory, Victorian Pier with arcades, family pub and Camera Obscura • Multiplex cinema, four theatres, seafront bandstand, indoor karting, 10-pin bowling, tennis, mini-golf, Dotto Train, speedway stadium.

☆ **Special Events:** **May:** Magnificent Motors. **June:** Classic Motorcycle Run, International Tennis Championships **July:** Emergency Services Display. **August:** International Air Show, Family Festival of Tennis, Tennis championships; South of England Tennis championships. **September:** MG South Downs Run. **October:** Victorian Festival, Beer Festival.

 Tourist Information Centre, Cornfield Road, Eastbourne BN21 4QA
0871 663 0031
e-mail: tic@eastbourne.gov.uk
www.visiteastbourne.com

🏖 **Beaches**

• BEACH. Five miles of beaches; shingle, sand and rockpools; promenade and pier with arcades, seafront cycleway; Dotto Train service; ample parking. *Safety and maintenance:* warning flags, lifeguards; Kidzone wristband scheme, first aid, rookie lifeguard classes. *Beach facilities:* deck chairs, sun loungers, parasols, beach huts, paddlecraft, water sports, boat trips, seafront bandstand, Punch & Judy; ice-cream kiosks, snack bars, restaurants and pubs; showers, toilets with ♿ access and baby changing facilities.

Falling Sands, Eastbourne

☆ Fun for all the Family ☆

◆ **1066 Battle Abbey and Battlefield, Battle (01424 773792).** Founded by William the Conqueror to commemorate the Battle of Hastings in 1066. The battle site, Abbey ruins and grounds are open to the public.

◆ **Bentley Wildfowl and Motor Museum, near Lewes (01825 840573).** Hundreds of waterfowl and wildlife, including flamingos, cranes and peacocks, in 23 acres.
www.bentley.org.uk

◆ **Bluebell Railway, near Uckfield (01825 720800).** Collection of veteran locos from 1865 to 1958. Trains steam through miles of Sussex countryside.
www.bluebellrailway.co.uk

◆ **Buckley's Yesterday's World, Battle (01424 775378).** Experience a day in a bygone age and explore the re-created shop and room displays. Children's activity areas, gift shop, teas.
www.yesterdaysworld.co.uk

◆ **Drusillas Park, Alfriston (01323 874100).** Collection of rare cattle, exotic flamingos, waterfowl, monkeys and parrots. Farm playground, miniature railway, shops.
www.drusillas.co.uk

◆ **Earnley Butterflies & Gardens, Near Chichester (01243 512637).** Walk amongst amazing tropical butterflies, stroll through themed gardens, and explore life as it used to be in the Nostalgia Museum.
www.earnleybutterfliesandgardens.co.uk

◆ **Paradise Park, Newhaven (01273 512123).** Journey through time and see how plants and animals lived 200 million years ago. Miniature railway, gnome settlement.
www.paradisepark.co.uk

◆ **Royal Pavilion, Brighton (01273 290900).** The former seaside palace of George IV, with lavish Chinese-style interiors. Shop and tearoom.
www.royalpavilion.org.uk

◆ **Sea Life Centre Brighton (01273 604234).** Come face to face with thousands of fascinating sea creatures. Restaurants and shops.
www.sealife.co.uk

◆ **Seven Sisters Sheep Centre, Near Eastbourne (01323 423302).** Over 40 breeds of sheep - help feed the lambs in Spring, see the sheep being milked, or take a ride on the tractor trailer. We'll be pleased to meet 'ewe'!
www.sheepcentre.co.uk

◆ **A Smuggler's Adventure, Hastings (01424 444412).** Relive the dangers and excitement that faced smugglers and customs men in times past. Displays and tableaux with life-sized figures .
www.smugglersadventure.co.uk

◆ **Weald and Downland Open Air Museum, near Chichester (01243 811363).** A collection of historic buildings, 16th century treadwheel etc saved from destruction. Heavy horses, shop, cafe.
www.wealddown.co.uk

Holidays

where the fun shines

Whatever you're seeking from your ideal family holiday in 2008, look no further than Bunn Leisure, here in glorious Selsey, West Sussex. We've got all your perfect holiday ingredients by the bucket and spade load... incredible family fun and entertainment, kids clubs for 0-16 year olds, swimming pools plus a wonderful beach on the Solent... and it's all just 90 minutes from London.

Family holidays from **£16***

All this is FREE

- ✔ Children's fun Clubs
- ✔ Live daytime and evening entertainment
- ✔ Swimming and Leisure Pools
- ✔ Multi-sports and play areas

- ✔ Fantastic value holidays
- ✔ 4 fabulous Holiday Parks
- ✔ Choice of accommodation
- ✔ 1 mile of beachfront

BUNN Leisure

Book today: 01243 606080

quote **CW1**

For more information visit **bunnleisure.co.uk**

*This offer is based on 6 people sharing Standard accommodation for a short break during our 2008 season and is only available on certain dates. Subject to availability. Visit web site for details

KENT

Best Beaches

 South East England Tourism
• Tel: 023 8062 5400
• Fax: 023 8062 0010
• e-mail: enquiries@tourismse.com
• www.visitsoutheastengland.com

A record number of beaches on the Kent coast have gained the prestigious Blue Flag Award for the highest standards of beach management and cleanliness. The family-friendly beach at Dymchurch has gained a Quality Coast Award.

BLUE FLAG BEACHES 2007

• *Herne Bay*
• *Birchington Minnis Bay*
• *Margate Main Sands*
• *Margate Westbrook Bay*
• *St Mildreds Bay, Westgate*
• *West Bay Westgate*
• *Botany Bay, Westgate*
• *Stone Bay, Broadstairs*
• *Tankerton*

For more information about holidaying in Kent see:
• www.visitkent.co.uk
• www.heartofkent.org.uk
• www.kentattractions.co.uk

BROADSTAIRS

⛼ Family Fun Activities: Ice-cream
parlours, amusement arcade, Pavilion with all-year entertainment, bandstand • Tennis, putting, golf course, crazy golf, bowls, angling • Award-winning St Peter's Village Tour • Skate park and climbing centre • Dickens House, Crampton Tower Museum.

☆ Special Events: **June:** Dickens Festival Week. **July:** Sea Sunday. **August:** Water Gala Day. Folk Week **September:** Open Bowls Tournament.

[i] **Visitor Information Centre, (in Dickens House Museum), 2 Victoria Parade, Broadstairs CT10 1QS**
0870 264 6111
e-mail: tourism@thanet.gov.uk
www.visitthanet.co.uk

⛿ Beaches

• VIKING BAY. Sandy beach, 150 metres long; promenade, harbour, pier and boardwalk, parking; ♿ access. *Safety and maintenance:* first-aid station, warning flags, animal logo signposts; lifeguards, bay inspector/information; cleaned daily. *Beach facilities:* deck chairs/sun loungers and chalets for hire, children's rides, donkey rides, Punch and Judy (August only), chalets for hire; pubs, cafes, shops and restaurants nearby, amusements, surfski/belly boards; lift to beach; toilets (toilets with ♿ RADAR key access Albion Road car park, Broadstairs Harbour, and Victoria Gardens). *Dog restrictions:* not permitted on beach 1 May to 30 September incl.

• STONE BAY. 200 metres long, sandy with chalk cliffs and rockpools; promenade; ♿ access. *Safety and maintenance:* cleaned daily. *Beach facilities:* chalets for hire. Cafes and restaurants nearby. Toilets. *Dog restrictions:* banned 15 May to 15 September between 10am and 6pm.

• LOUISA BAY. 150 metres long, quiet sandy bay; promenade. Disabled access via failry steep slope. *Safety and maintenance:* warning signs; beach cleaned daily. *Beach facilities:* chalets for hire; cafe, tidal pool. *Dog restrictions:* "poop scoop" beach.

• JOSS BAY. 200 metres long, sandy beach, parking, ♿ access. *Safety and maintenance:* warning flags, lifeguards; cleaned daily; animal logo signposts to help children find their way back to parents. *Beach facilities:* deck chairs for hire, surf skis/belly boards; lessons; cafe; toilets with ♿ RADAR key access Easter-Sep. *Dog restrictions:* "poop scoop" beach.

• KINGSGATE BAY. 150 metres long; quiet and secluded sandy beach. *Safety and maintenance:* cleaned daily. *Beach facilities:* chalets for hire; clifftop pub. *Dog restrictions:* "poop scoop" beach.

• BOTANY BAY. 200 metres long, sandy beach; ♿ access. *Safety and maintenance:* lifeguards/bay inspector; warnings, cleaned daily. *Beach facilities:* cafe, clifftop pub; toilets. *Dog restrictions:* dog ban May-Sep.

• DUMPTON GAP. Quiet sandy bay with some rocks, 150 metres long; promenade and parking. Disabled access. *Safety and maintenance:* warning signs; cleaned daily. *Beach facilities:* chalets for hire; cafe; toilets. *Dog restrictions:* "poop scoop" beach.

MARGATE

⛼ Family Fun Activities: Heated
indoor leisure pool, indoor sports/leisure centre, amusement arcades • Shell Grotto, The Droit House, Margate Museum • Windmill, lifeboat station • Ten-pin bowling, bowls, indoor bowls, tennis, putting, pitch and putt, golf course, mini-golf, crazy golf, adventure golf, angling • Casino, theatres, nightclubs, disco, bandstand.

☆ **Special Events:** June: Great Bucket & Spade Run. June/July: Open Bowls Tournament, Kent Air Show. August: Carnival Parade.

ⓘ **Visitor Information Centre, 12-13 The Parade, Margate CT9 1EY**
0870 264 6111
e-mail: tourism@thanet.gov.uk
www.visitthanet.co.uk

Beaches

• MARGATE MAIN SANDS. 200 metres long, sandy beach, promenade and boardwalk, parking, ♿ access. *Safety and maintenance:* warning flags, animal logo signposts to help children find their way back to parents, first-aid station, lifeguards and lifeboat; bay inspector/ information, beach cleaned daily. *Beach facilities:* sun loungers, deckchairs for hire; tidal boating pool, paddlecraft, donkey rides; kiddies' corner; cafes, restaurants, pubs; toilets with ♿ access. *Dog restrictions:* not permitted on beach 1 May to 30 September incl.

• PALM BAY/HODGES GAP & FORENESS POINT. 200 metres long; sandy, sheltered beach, parking. *Safety and maintenance:* cleaned daily. *Beach facilities:* designated water-ski area; toilets. *Dog restrictions:* "poop scoop" beach.

• WALPOLE BAY. Sandy beach 400 metres long, popular watersports bay, tidal pool, lift, promenade, parking, ♿ access. *Safety and maintenance:* warning flags, lifeguards; cleaned daily. *Beach facilities:* chalets and jet skis for hire; cafe, toilets. *Dog restrictions:* dog ban 1 May to 30 September incl.

• WESTBROOK BAY. 200 metres long, sandy; promenade and parking. *Safety and maintenance:* warning flags, lifeguards, bay inspector/information; first-aid station; cleaned daily. *Beach facilities:* deck chairs, chalets for hire; designated water ski area; children's fun park; cafe; toilets with ♿ access. *Dog restrictions:* banned from 15 May to 15 September 10am to 6pm.

RAMSGATE

⛴ **Family Fun Activities:** Heated indoor leisure pool, sports and leisure centre • Maritime museum • Royal harbour and yacht marina • Amusement arcades, leisure park and boating pool, tennis, bowls, angling • Theatre, cinema, discos.

☆ **Special Events:** July: Powerboat and Waterski Grand Prix, Carnival Parade, Costumed Walks. August: Open Bowls Tournament, International Sailing Week. September: Model Ships Rally.

ⓘ **Visitor Information Centre, 17 Albert Court, York Street, Ramsgate CT11 9DN**
0870 264 6111
e-mail: tourism@thanet.gov.uk
www.visitthanet.co.uk

Beaches

• MAIN SANDS. Popular sandy beach, 250 metres long; promenade and parking, ♿ access. *Safety and maintenance:* animal logo signposts to help children find their way back to their parents, warning flags, lifeguards, bay inspector/information; first-aid station; beach cleaned daily. *Beach facilities:* donkey rides; deck chairs, sun loungers for hire; amusements, children's play area; cafes, restaurants, pubs, shops; toilets with ♿ access; Edwardian lift to beach. *Dog restrictions:* not permitted on beach 1 May to 30 September incl.

• PEGWELL BAY. A stretch of unprotected sea cliffs with great geological interest. Part of Kent's largest national Nature Reserve. Toilets, cafe, picnic area, parking.

☆ Fun for all the Family ☆

◆ **A Day at the Wells, Royal Tunbridge Wells (01892 546545)**. Experience the sights and sounds of 18th century Tunbridge Wells. Special commentary for children.

◆ **Canterbury Tales, Canterbury (01227 479227)**. Chaucer's 14th century tales brought vividly to life by the latest audio-visual technology.
www.canterburytales.org.uk

◆ **Eagle Heights, Eynsford (01322 866577)**. One of the UK's largest bird of prey centres with over 50 species of raptors. Daily flying demonstrations, and collection of reptiles and mammals.
www.eagleheights.co.uk

◆ **Finchcocks, Goudhurst (01580 211702)**. Living museum of early keyboard instruments, played whenever the house is open.
www.finchcocks.co.uk

◆ **Historic Dockyard, Chatham (01634 823800)**. Step back 200 years at the world's most complete Georgian dockyard, now a living museum. New permanent lifeboat exhibition.
www.chdt.org.uk

◆ **The Hop Farm at the Kentish Oast Village, Paddock Wood (0870 0274166)**. Exhibitions and displays of hop picking and shop life in Victorian times. Indoor and outdoor play areas, animal farm and pets' corner.
www.thehopfarm.co.uk

◆ **Howletts Wild Animal Park, near Canterbury (01303 264647)**. Caged and free-roaming animals including tigers and gorillas. Teas, picnics.
www.howletts.net

◆ **Kent and East Sussex Steam Railway** operates 80-minute steam train rides from Tenterden Town Station to Northiam (**01580 765155**).
www.kesr.org.uk

◆ **Museum of Kent Life, Cobtree (01622 763936)**. History of the county in displays and live exhibits. Rare breeds and farm animals; play area.
www.museum-kentlife.co.uk

◆ **Romney, Hythe and Dymchurch Railway (01797 362353)**. Runs from Hythe to Dungeness – 80 minute journey through beautiful landscape.
www.rhdr.org.uk

◆ **South of England Rare Breeds Centre, Ashford (01233 861493)**. Set in 120 acres of unspoilt countryside - friendly farm animals, indoor and outdoor play areas, Discovery Garden.
www.rarebreeds.org.uk

◆ **Wingham Bird Park, near Canterbury (01227 720836)**. Set in 25 acres of beautiful countryside, with large walk-through aviaries, reptile house, adventure playground.

LONDON & HOME COUNTIES

ⓘ Visit London
1 Warwick Row, London SW1E 5ER
• Tel: 020 7932 2000
• Fax: 020 7932 0222
e-mail: enquiries@visitlondon.com
• www.visitlondon.com
  www.kidslovelondon.com

HISTORIC BUILDINGS

◆ **Hampton Court, East Molesey, Surrey (020 8781 9500).** Built over 400 years ago, this became one of Henry VIII's royal palaces. Tudor tennis court, Great Vine and Maze. Nearest BR station: Hampton Court.

◆ **Houses of Parliament and Strangers' Gallery**: if you wish to listen to a debate apply in advance to your MP or join the queue at St Stephen's Entrance on the day.

◆ **Kensington Palace (0870 751 5170).** State Apartments of the late Stuart and Hanoverian periods containing 17th century furniture and pictures. Nearest Tube: Queensway.

◆ **St Paul's Cathedral (020 7246 8348).** Sir Christopher Wren's masterpiece built between 1675 and 1710. Nearest Tube: St Paul's, Mansion House.

◆ **Tower of London (020 7709 0765).** Built by William the Conqueror as a fortress, this magnificent building today houses the Crown Jewels. Nearest Tube: Tower Hill.

◆ **Westminster Abbey (020 7222 7110).** Founded by Edward the Confessor in 1065, the Abbey has become the burial place of many famous people. Nearest Tube: Westminster.

MUSEUMS & GALLERIES

British Museum (020 7323 8000).
Imperial War Museum (020 7416 5000).
Museum of London (020 7600 3699).
National Gallery (020 7839 3321).
National Maritime Museum (020 8858 4422).
National Portrait Gallery (020 7312 2463).
Natural History Museum (020 7942 5000).
Royal Academy of Arts (020 7300 8000).
Science Museum (020 7938 8000).
Tate Britain (020 7887 8008).
Tate Modern (020 7887 8734).
Victoria & Albert Museum (020 7942 2197).

◆ **Bethnal Green Museum of Childhood (020 8983 5200).** A child's world of toys, dolls, dolls' houses, children's costumes.
www.museumofchildhood.org.uk

London Dungeon (020 7403 7221). The world's first medieval horror exhibition featuring gruesome scenes of torture, murder and depravation. Perfect for the kids! Nearest Tube: London Bridge.
www.dungeons.co.uk

London Transport Museum (020 7379 6344). A collection of historic vehicles illustrating the development of London's transport system. Nearest Tube: Covent Garden.
www.ltmuseum.co.uk

VISITOR ATTRACTIONS

British Airways London Eye, South Bank, London (0870 5000 600). Stunning views over Central London and beyond during a half-hour ride on the gently moving 135m high observational wheel.
www.londoneye.com

Chessington World of Adventures (0870 444 7777). Exciting theme areas, rides, circus and zoo – a world of adventure for all the family. BR: Chessington South.
www.chessington.com

Cutty Sark, Greenwich Pier (020 8858 3445). This famous clipper ship built for the tea trade contains a fine collection of figureheads and seafaring relics.
www.cuttysark.org.uk

HMS Belfast (020 7940 6328). The last survivor of the Royal Navy's big ships, now a permanent floating museum. Nearest Tube: London Bridge.
www.iwm.org.uk/belfast

Kew Gardens, near Richmond (020 8332 5655). 300 acres, once belonging to the Royal family, now contains 25000 different plant species; greenhouses, herbarium and museums. Tube: Kew Gardens.
www.rbgkew.org.uk

Legoland, Windsor (08705 040404). A theme park with a difference, all set in 150 acres of wooded parkland.
www.lego.com

London Zoo (020 7722 3333). One of the largest zoos in the world containing a varied collection of animals, birds, reptiles and insects. New Children's Zoo tells how people and animals live side by side. Nearest Tube: Camden Town.
www.londonzoo.co.uk

Madame Tussaud's (0870 400 3000). The world famous waxworks of contemporary and historic figures complete with the inevitable Chamber of Horrors. Nearest Tube: Baker Street.
www.madame-tussauds.com

Royal Observatory, Greenwich (020 8858 4422). Includes Wren's Flamsteed House, Meridian Building and Planetarium. New high precision pendulum clock donated by Moscow Research Centre.
www.nmm.ac.uk

London Planetarium (0870 400 3000). The story of the stars and planets told by means of an elaborate and intriguing projection system. Nearest Tube: Baker Street.
www.london-planetarium.com

Thames Barrier (020 8305 4188). Multi-media exhibition tells the story of the city's defence against floods. Can also be visited by boat.

FREE AND REDUCED RATE HOLIDAY VISITS!
Don't miss our
Readers' Offer Vouchers
on pages 9-44

Stavrou Hotels

Gower Hotel

129 SUSSEX GARDENS,
HYDE PARK, LONDON W2 2RX
Tel: 0207 262 2262
Fax: 0207 262 2006
e-mail: gower@stavrouhotels.co.uk
www.stavrouhotels.co.uk

The Gower Hotel is a small family-run Hotel, centrally located, within two minutes' walk from Paddington Station, which benefits from the Heathrow Express train "15 minutes to and from Heathrow Airport". Excellently located for sightseeing London's famous sights and shops, Hyde Park, Madame Tussaud's, Oxford Street, Harrods, Marble Arch, Buckingham Palace and many more close by. All rooms have private shower and WC, radio, TV (includes satellite and video channels), direct dial telephone and tea and coffee facilities. All recently refurbished and fully centrally heated. 24 hour reception.

All prices are inclusive of a large traditional English Breakfast & VAT

Single Rooms from £30-£79 • Double/Twin Rooms from £60-£89 •Triple & Family Rooms from £80
• Discount available on 3 nights or more if you mention this advert

Queens Hotel

33 Anson Road, Tufnell Park,
LONDON N7
Tel: 0207 607 4725
Fax: 0207 697 9725
e-mail: queens@stavrouhotels.co.uk
www.stavrouhotels.co.uk

The Queens Hotel is a large double-fronted Victorian building standing in its own grounds five minutes' walk from Tufnell Park Station. Quietly situated with ample car parking spaces; 15 minutes to West End and close to London Zoo, Hampstead and Highgate. Two miles from Kings Cross and St Pancras Stations. Many rooms en suite. **All prices include full English Breakfast plus VAT. Children at reduced prices. Discounts on longer stays.**

Single Rooms from £30-£55 • Double/Twin Rooms from £40-£69 •Triple & Family Rooms from £20 per person

Stavrou Hotels is a family-run group of hotels.

We offer quality and convenience at affordable rates.

A VERY WARM WELCOME AWAITS YOU

Our hotels accept all major Credit cards, but some charges may apply.

Looking for holiday accommodation?
search for details of properties where children are welcome
www.holidayguides.com

 # The Athena

110-114 SUSSEX GARDENS, HYDE PARK, LONDON W2 1UA

Tel: 0207 706 3866 • Fax: 0207 262 6143

e-mail: athena@stavrouhotels.co.uk • www.stavrouhotels.co.uk

TREAT YOURSELVES TO A QUALITY HOTEL AT AFFORDABLE PRICES

The Athena is a newly completed family run hotel in a restored Victorian building. Professionally designed, including a lift to all floors and exquisitely decorated, we offer our clientele the ambience and warm hospitality necessary for a relaxing and enjoyable stay. Ideally located in a beautiful tree-lined avenue, extremely well-positioned for sightseeing London's famous sights and shops; Hyde Park, Madame Tussaud's, Oxford Street, Marble Arch, Knightsbridge, Buckingham Palace and many more are all within walking distance.

Travel connections to all over London are excellent, with Paddington and Lancaster Gate Stations, Heathrow Express, A2 Airbus and buses minutes away.
Our tastefully decorated bedrooms have en suite bath/shower rooms, satellite colour TV, bedside telephones, tea/coffee making facilities. Hairdryers, trouser press, laundry and ironing facilities available on request. Car parking available.

Stavrou Hotels is a family run group of hotels.
We offer quality and convenience at affordable rates.
A VERY WARM WELCOME AWAITS YOU.

Single Rooms from £50-£89
Double/Twin Rooms from £64-£99
Triple & Family Rooms from £25 per person
All prices include full English breakfast plus VAT.

Our hotels accept all major Credit cards, but some charges may apply.

EAST ANGLIA

Best Beaches

A very impressive total of 14 beaches in this area were proud winners in 2007 of the European Blue Flag for beaches meeting the strictest of standards. Several beaches also were proud winners of a Quality Coast Award.

i East of England Tourism
Bedfordshire, Cambridgeshire, Essex, Hertfordshire, Norfolk, Suffolk).
• Tel: 01284 727470
• Fax: 01284 706657
• e-mail: info@eet.ork.uk
• www.visiteastofengland.com

BLUE FLAG BEACHES 2007
• *Dovercourt Bay*
• *Southend*
  Shoebury Common
  Shoeburyness
  Three Shells Beach
• *Cromer*
• *Gorleston*
• *Mundesley*
• *Sea Palling*
• *Sheringham*
• *Lowestoft*
  North
  South of Pier
• *Southwold Pier*
• *Felixstowe South*
• *Brightlingsea*

For more information about holidaying in East Anglia see:
• *www.visitbeds-luton.com* • *www.midbeds.gov.uk* • *www.bedford.gov.uk*
• *wwww.vistcambridge.org*
• *wwww.essex-sunshine-coast.org.uk* • *www.realessex.co.uk*
• *wwww.hertfordshire.com*
• *wwww.visitnorfolk.co.uk www.northnorfolk.org*
• *wwww.visit-suffolk.org.uk* • *www.visitsuffolkattractions.co.uk*

CLACTON-ON-SEA

⌂ Family Fun Activities: Fun-packed pier with rides, amusements, cafes and fishing (wheelchair accessible) • Leisure centre with swimming pool • Two theatres, cinema, bingo, night clubs • Clacton Factory Shopping Village.

ⓘ Tourist Information Centre, **Town Hall, Station Road, Clacton-on-Sea CO15 1SE • 01255 686633** e-mail: emorgan@tendringdc.gov.uk www.essex-sunshine-coast.org.uk

⛰ Beaches

• BEACH. Long sandy beach, gently sloping. *Beach facilities:* deck chairs, beach cafes; toilets. *Dog restrictions:* dogs banned on some beaches during main holiday season.

SOUTHEND

⌂ Family Fun Activities: Pier (longest pleasure pier in the world), Sea Life Adventure, Cliffs Pavilion, Adventure Island • Sailing, water ski-ing, windsurfing, motor boats, marine activity centre • Indoor swimming pools, skateboard park, tennis, bowls, golf, miniature golf, putting, children's playgrounds • Museums, planetarium, art gallery; theatres, nightclubs, discos • The Kursaal indoor entertainments centre

ⓘ Visitor Information Centre, **Southend Pier, Western Esplanade, Southend-on-Sea SS1 1EE 01702 215120 • Fax: 01702 431449** www.visitsouthend.co.uk

⛰ Beaches

• BEACHES. 7 miles of sea and foreshore with sand and shingle beach, stretching from Shoeburyness to Chalkwell and Leigh; ample parking. *Safety and maintenance:* cleaned daily boards with information on bathing water quality. *Beach facilities:* paddling pool, activity frame, beach shower; cafes, restaurants; toilets. *Dog restrictions:* from 1st May to 30th September must be kept on a lead on promenade.

GREAT YARMOUTH

⌂ Family Fun Activities: Marina Leisure Centre, Hollywood Indoor Golf, Pleasure Beach, Sea Life Centre, House of Wax, Model Village, Joyland Fun Park, "Amazonia" The Jungle at the Winter gardens - children's adventure play.• Stock car racing, greyhound racing, horse racing, golf; putting, pitch and putt, outdoor bowls, ten-pin bowling, petanque, indoor karting • Marina, boating, fishing, sea cruises, Broads cruises, horse riding, indoor swimming pools, squash, tennis amusement arcades, children's playgrounds, Pirates' Cove (novelty golf), piers, road train • Museums, theatres, circus, cinema, nightclubs.

☆ **Special Events:** Fireworks Displays, Herring Festival, Festival of Bowls, Maritime Festival. Carnivals and fêtes, band concerts.

ⓘ Tourist Information Centre, 25 **Marine Parade, Great Yarmouth NR30 2EN • 01493 836346** tourism@great-yarmouth.gov.uk www.great-yarmouth.co.uk

FREE AND REDUCED RATE HOLIDAY VISITS!
Don't miss our Readers' Offer Vouchers on pages 9-44

Beaches.

- GREAT YARMOUTH BEACH. Sandy beach, five miles long; two piers with entertainment. *Safety and maintenance:* warning flags, lifeguards; cleaned regularly. *Beach facilities:* deck chairs, windbreaks, beach huts; trampolines, donkey rides, inflatables, horse drawn landaus, pleasure boat trips; ice-cream kiosks, snack bars, restaurants and pubs; toilets on sea front with & access. *Dog restrictions:* banned from beach during main season.

- GORLESTON BEACH. One and a half miles long, sandy; promenade and pier with good parking adjacent. *Safety and maintenance:* warning flags, lifeguards; beach cleaned during summer season. *Beach facilities*: deck chairs, trampolines, beach huts and chalets; ice-cream kiosks, snack bars, restaurants and pubs; toilets with & access. *Dog restrictions:* banned from Blue Flag section during main summer months.

LOWESTOFT

Family Fun Activities: Mayhem soft play area, museums, pier; swimming pool, indoor football centre, adventure golf, golf, putting, pitch and putt, tennis, bowling, horse riding, water sports, parks with children's playgrounds • Theatres, cinemas, discos, nightclubs. Nearby: New Pleasurewood Hills, Suffolk Wildlife Park, Transport Museum, Lowestoft Ness (Britain's most easterly point).

i Tourist Information Centre,
East Point Pavilion, Royal Plain,
Lowestoft NR33 0AP • 01502 533600
e-mail: touristinfo@waveney.gov.uk
www.visit-lowestoft.co.uk
Brochure info line: 0870 6061303

Beaches

- KESSINGLAND BEACH. Pebble and shingle with some sand; low cliffs, easy access. *Safety and maintenance:* cleaned by Local Authority. *Dog restrictions:* banned from 1st May to 30th September; must be kept on lead on promenade.

- PAKEFIELD BEACH. Sandy beach with some shingle below low grassy cliffs; parking. *Safety and maintenance:* cleaned by Local Authority; dangerous to clamber or swim near groynes. *Beach facilities:* pubs; toilets with & access.

- LOWESTOFT RESORT BEACHES. Sandy pleasure beaches with two piers; esplanade and ample parking. *Safety and maintenance:* warning flags, lifeguards; dangerous to clamber or swim near groynes; cleaned daily. *Beach facilities:* children's corner, chalets, ice-cream kiosks, restaurants, snack bars, pubs; toilets with & access. *Dog restrictions:* banned from 1st May to 30th September; must be kept on lead on promenade.

- SOUTHWOLD RESORT BEACH. Part sand, part shingle with sand dunes; refurbished pier including amusements and refreshments. Parking. *Safety and maintenance:* warning flags, lifeguards; cleaned by Local Authority. *Beach facilities:* beach huts; cafes, pubs; toilets. *Dog restrictions:* banned from 1st May to 30th September; must be kept on lead on promenade.

- SOUTHWOLD DENES. Part sand, part shingle with sand dunes. This rural beach is secluded and peaceful, an ideal place for walkers and nature enthusiasts. Parking. *Safety and maintenance:* cleaned by Local Authority.

☆ Fun for all the Family ☆

BEDFORDSHIRE

◆ **Whipsnade Wild Animal Park, Dunstable (01582 872171).** Britain's largest conservation centre specialising in breeding certain endangered species. Children's zoo, steam railway.
www.whipsnade.co.uk

◆ **Woburn Safari Park (01525 290407).** Britain's largest drive-through safari park. Roundabouts and rides.
www.woburnsafari.co.uk

CAMBRIDGESHIRE

◆ **Nene Valley Railway, Peterborough (01780 784444).** A preserved steam railway with 7½ miles of track. Cafe shop, museum and engine shed.
www.nvr.org.uk

◆ **Sacrewell Farm and Country Centre, Thornaugh (01780 782254).** 500-acre farm with working watermill, nature trails, displays of farming bygones.
www.sacrewell.org.uk

ESSEX

◆ **Colchester Zoo, Colchester (01206 331292).** World-wide collection of animals and birds, with daily displays of parrots, sealions and falcons. Penguin parade, snake handling, meet the elephants.
www.colchester-zoo.co.uk

HERTFORDSHIRE

◆ **Paradise Wildlife Park, Broxbourne (01992 470490).** 17 acres with lots of animals; woodland railway, pony rides, aviary, education centre.
www.pwpark.com

NORFOLK

◆ **Banham Zoo, Banham (01953 887771).** Over 25 acres of wildlife in parkland setting with extensive collection of rare and endangered species. Road train, adventure playground and World of Penguins.
www.banhamzoo.co.uk

◆ **Dinosaur Adventure Park, Weston Longville (01603 876310).** Walk through woodland to view dinosaurs in natural settings. Adventure rides, play area, wooded maze; bygones museum.
www.dinosaurpark.co.uk

◆ **Sea Life Centre, Great Yarmouth (01493 330631).** A spectacular way to experience the underwater world, with themed tanks on local marine life.
www.sealife.co.uk

SUFFOLK

◆ **Easton Farm Park, Wickham Market (01728 746475).** Victorian farm setting for many species of farm animals including rare breeds. Nature trail, pets paddock and adventure playground.

◆ **Pleasurewood Hills Family Theme Park, Lowestoft (01502 586000).** Live shows and all the rides your family can handle! Off A12 between Great Yarmouth and Lowestoft.
www.pleasurewoodhills.co.uk

◆ **Suffolk Wildlife Park, Kessingland (01502 740291).** Suffolk's "walking safari" set in 100 acres of dramatic coastal parkland. Daily feeding sessions, safari road train, adventure playground.
www.suffolkwildlifepark.co.uk

High House Farm ETC ◆◆◆

Cransford, Framlingham, Woodbridge IP13 9PD
Tel: 01728 663461 * Fax: 01728 663409
e-mail: b&b@highhousefarm.co.uk
www.highhousefarm.co.uk

Exposed oak beams • inglenook fireplaces • one double room, en suite and one large family room with double and twin beds and private adjacent bathroom • children's cots • high chairs • books • toys • outside play equipment • attractive semi-moated gardens • farm and woodland walks.
Explore the heart of rural Suffolk, local vineyards, Easton Farm Park, Framlingham and Orford Castles, Parham Air Museum, Saxtead Windmill, Minsmere, Snape Maltings, Woodland Trust and the Heritage Coast.
Bed and Breakfast from £25. Reductions for children and stays of three nights or more.

CASTAWAYS HOLIDAY PARK

BH & HPA approved

Set in the quiet, peaceful village of Bacton, with direct access to fine sandy beach, and ideal for beach fishing and discovering Norfolk and The Broads. Modern Caravans, Pine Lodges and Flats with all amenities. Licensed Club. Entertainment. Amusement Arcade. Children's Play Area.

PETS WELCOME

on-line booking facility available

Enquiries and Bookings to:
**Castaways Holiday Park, Paston Road, Bacton-on-Sea, Norfolk NR12 0JB • Tel: (01692) 650436 and 650418
www.castawaysholidaypark.co.uk**

Located on a working farm, a courtyard of 2/3 bedroomed converted stables, 3 converted barns and 2 cottages, all fully equipped. Sleeps up to 10. Ideally situated for the beautiful North Norfolk coast, Sandringham, Norwich, and The Broads. 365 acres of mature woodland adjoining farm – private fishing in owners' lake. Indoor heated swimming Pool. Pets welcome at a charge of £10.
**MOOR FARM STABLE COTTAGES,
FOXLEY, NORFOLK NR20 4QP • Tel or Fax: 01362 688523
e-mail: enquiry@moorfarmstablecottages.co.uk
www.moorfarmstablecottages.co.uk**

Looking for holiday accommodation?
search for details of properties where children are welcome
www.holidayguides.com

MIDLANDS

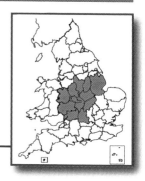

 Best Beaches

Three beaches in the East Midlands area have attained the standards necessary to have won a Blue Flag for 2007.

BLUE FLAG BEACHES 2007
- *Mablethorpe*
- *Skegness*
- *Sutton on Sea*

For more information about holidaying in the Midlands see:
- www.glos-cotswolds.com
- www.visitherefordshire.co.uk
- www.shropshiretourism.info
- www.enjoystaffordshire.com
- www.visitnorthernwarwickshire.com
- www.visitshakespeare-country.co.uk
- www.worcestershire-tourism.org

☆ Fun for all the Family ☆

DERBYSHIRE

◆ **Gulliver's Kingdom, Matlock Bath.** (01925 444888). Theme park set in 15 acres of wooded hillside, designed especially for younger children.
www.gulliversfun.co.uk

◆ **Heights of Abraham, Matlock Bath.** (01629 582365). Spectacular cable car ride to hilltop country park. Show caverns, visitor centre, restaurant.
www.heights-of-abraham.co.uk

◆ **National Tramway Museum, Crich.** (01773 854321). Tramcars from all over the world; scenic displays, restaurant, children's playground.
www.tramway.co.uk

GLOUCESTERSHIRE

◆ **National Waterways Museum, Gloucester.** (01452 318200). Recreates the story of Britain's inland waterways. Working machinery, demonstrations.
www.nwm.org.uk

◆ **Slimbridge Wildfowl and Wetlands Centre, Slimbridge** (01453 891900). Over 2300 birds of 180 different species, including in winter wild swans, geese and ducks. Activities throughout the year.
www.wwt.org.uk

◆ **Sudeley Castle, Winchcombe.** (01242 602308). Toys, treasures, peacock gardens, children's play area. Katherine Parr (Henry VIII's Queen) buried here.
www.sudeleycastle.co.uk

LEICESTERSHIRE

◆ **Moira Furnace & Craft Workshops, Near Ashby de la Zouch.** (01283 224667). Impressive 19th century blast furnace museum. Woodland walks, nature trail, children's play area.

◆ **Snibston Discovery Park, Coalville.** (01530 278444). Exhibition hall with 5 galleries exploring the county's industrial heritage, plus outdoor science play area, colliery tours.

LINCOLNSHIRE

◆ **Natureland Seal Sanctuary, Skegness** (01754 764345). Entertainment, education and conservation: baby seals, penguins, free-flight tropical birds, plus lots of other fascinating creatures.
www.skegnessnatureland.co.uk

◆ **National Fishing Heritage Centre, Grimsby** (01472 323345). Tells the story of fishermen, their boats and the waters they fished in; the dangers and hardships of life at sea are explained.
www.nelincs.gov.uk

NORTHAMPTONSHIRE

◆ **Turner's Musical Merry-go-round, Queen Eleanor Vale, Newport Pagnell Road, Wootton** (01604 763314). Indoor fairground with historic and functioning fairground organs, rides on giant roundabout.

NOTTINGHAMSHIRE

◆ **Sherwood Forest Country Park and Visitor Centre, Near Mansfield** (01623 823202). Includes visitor centre with Robin Hood Exhibition, guided walks, picnic sites, and refreshments.
www.robinhood.co.uk

◆ **Tales of Robin Hood, Nottingham.** (0115 9483284). The latest audio-visual technology transports you through 700 years of history as you ride through Medieval Nottingham.
www.robinhood.uk.com

☆ Fun for all the Family ☆

OXFORDSHIRE

◈ **Blenheim Palace, Woodstock (08700 602080).** Home of the Duke of Marlborough, with magnificent collection of tapestries and porcelain. Landscaped grounds with butterfly house, adventure playground and railway. World Heritage Site.
www.blenheimpalace.com

◈ **Cotswold Wild Life Park, Burford (01993 823006).** A large and varied collection of animals from all over the world in natural surroundings.
www.cotswoldwildlifepark.co.uk

SHROPSHIRE

◈ **Ironbridge Gorge Museum, Telford (01952 432166).** Award-winning museum complex which brings industrial history to life. Working museums and real history - the images and objects of the industrial revolution.
www.ironbridge.org.uk

◈ **Hoo Farm Animal Kingdom, near Telford (01952 677917).** Friendly llamas, inquisitive ostriches, plus lots more. Undercover and outdoor attractions.
www.hoofarm.com

STAFFORDSHIRE

◈ **Alton Towers, Alton (0870 444 4455).** Europe's premier leisure park – rides, gardens, monorail, shops, adventure play areas etc. New interactive adventure ride – Duel.
www.alton-towers.co.uk

◈ **Drayton Manor Theme Park and Zoo, Near Tamworth. (01827 287979).** Over 100 heart stopping range of rides, including Apocalypse, Shockwave and Stormforce 10; nature trail, zoo, parkland and lakes.
www.draytonmanor.co.uk

WARWICKSHIRE

◈ **Heritage Motor Centre, Gaydon (01926 641188).** Purpose-built transport museum containing collection of historic British cars. Site includes four-wheel drive circuit.
www.heritage.org.uk

◈ **The Shakespearian Properties, Stratford-upon-Avon (01789 204016).** Five distinctive homes including Shakespeare's Birthplace and Anne Hathaway's Cottage, all administered by the Shakespeare Birthplace Trust.
www.stratford-upon-avon.co.uk

◈ **Warwick Castle, Warwick (0870 442 2000).** Britain's greatest medieval experience – castle with dungeon, armoury and torture chamber, all set in 60 acres of grounds.
www.warwick-castle.co.uk

WEST MIDLANDS

◈ **National Sea Life Centre, Birmingham (0121-633 4700).** Bringing the magic of the marine world to the heart of Birmingham with over 55 displays of marine and freshwater creatures. Features the world's first 360° fully transparent viewing tunnel.
www.sealife.co.uk

◈ **Thinktank at Millennium Point, Birmingham (0121 202 2222).** 10 themed galleries where you can examine the past, investigate the present, and explore what the future may bring.
www.thinktank.ac

WORCESTERSHIRE

◈ **West Midland Safari & Leisure Park, Spring Grove (01299 402114).** From reptiles to roller coasters – it's all here!
www.wmsp.co.uk

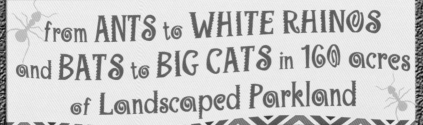

Woodland Hills Court
Holiday Cottages

We have 5 newly built holiday cottages which will be available from November 2007.

The cottages are brick built. Four have two double/ twin bedrooms, one of which is wheelchair-friendly. The fifth cottage has one bedroom with a 4-poster bed and a bathroom with a roll-topped bath. All five cottages have an open-plan, well equipped kitchen, dining room and lounge with colour TV and DVD player. The four two-bedroom cottages have a modern, good-sized wet room. There are gardens and patios for each cottage for added privacy, and full use of a drying and laundry room for our guests.

- All linen and towels are provided.
- A child's cot is available on request.
- Electricity is extra, each cottage having its own meter.
- There is ample off road parking.

South Derbyshire offers lots of entertainment for all ages, Donington Park motor racing, Alton Towers, Calke Abbey, Kedleston Hall, Twycross Zoo, and lots more in the new National Forest, including horse riding.

A starter pack will be placed in your cottage; flowers and/or chocolates arranged on request.

Price from £350 to £500 per week
Short stays subject to availability,
priced at £250 for a 4 night stay.

**Woodland Hills Court
Ivy House Farm
Stanton by Bridge
Derby DE73 7HT
Tel: 01332 863152
info@ivy-house-farm.com
www.ivy-house-farm.com**

NORTH-EAST ENGLAND

Best Beaches

This year no less than 15 beaches on this impressive stretch of coastline have won a European Blue Flag. Several beaches have also gained a Quality Coast Award.

 North East England Tourism
- Tel: 01904 707961
- Fax: 01904 707070
- www.visitnortheastengland.com

Blue Flag Beaches 2007
- *Tynemouth*
  King Edward's Bay
  Longsands South
- *Roker*
- *Seaburn*
- *South Shields, Sandhaven*
- *Whitby West Cliff*
- *Filey*
- *Scarborough North Bay*
- *Bridlington North*
- *Bridlington South*
- *Hornsea*
- *Whitley Bay South*
- *Withernsea*
- *Cleethorpes Central*
- *Seaton Carew Foreshore*

For more information about holidaying in the North East see:
www.visitteesvalley.co.uk
www.visitnorthumberland.com
www.visitcountydurham.com
www.visitnewcastlegasteshead.co.uk

BRIDLINGTON

☷ Family Fun Activities: Summer
shows • Children's attractions • Sports and games, golf, boating, fishing, wind-surfing • Indoor Leisure World (4 pools). New: Eye of the Bay (big wheel)

☆ Special Events: May: Week-long
festival of street and theatre shows. **August:** Lions Carnival. **September:** Sea angling week. **October:** Carnival Championships.

ℹ️ **Information Centre, 25 Prince Street, Bridlington YO15 2NP • 01262 673474**
www.discoveryorkshirecoast.com
www.visitbrid.co.uk
www.visiteastyorkshire.com

⛰ Beaches

• NORTH BEACH. Two miles long, sandy and naturally sheltered, with cliffs and rock pools towards northern end. Promenade; good parking. *Safety and maintenance:* cleaned daily. *Beach facilities:* deck chairs; various entertainments on beach; ice cream kiosks, snack bars, restaurants and pubs; toilets with ♿ access. *Dog restrictions:* banned May to end September, must be kept on lead on Promenade.

• SOUTH BEACH. Two miles long, sandy and naturally sheltered with some dunes at southern end. Promenade and good parking. *Safety and maintenance:* cleaned daily. *Beach facilities:* deck chairs; beach chalets for hire; beach activities; donkey rides; ice cream kiosks, snack bars, restaurants and pubs; toilets with ♿ access (open 24 hours in summer). *Dog restrictions:* banned May to end September, must be kept on lead on Promenade.

CLEETHORPES

☷ Family Fun Activities: Leisure
Centre, Pleasure Island Theme Park, Cleethorpes Coast Light Railway, Discovery Centre, The Jungle Zoo; 10-Pin Bowling Centre, Promenade Gardens, Lakeside Sand Pit and Paddling Pool, Fantasy World; Laser Adventure • Crazy golf, amusement arcades, children's entertainment, night clubs, discos.

☆ Special Events: May: Kite Festival.
July/August: Carnival Week and Parade. Markets: Wednesday and Sunday.

ℹ️ **Tourist Information Centre, 42/43 Alexandra Road, Cleethorpes DN35 8LE 01472 323111 • Fax: 01472 323112 e-mail: cleetic@nelincs.gov.uk www.nelincs.gov.uk/tourism**

⛰ Beaches

• NORTH PROMENADE. Sandy and naturally sheltered; promenade; good parking. *Safety and maintenance:* Beach Safety Officers; sandbanks; beach cleaned daily. *Beach facilities:* deck chairs; donkeys, swings, Big Wheel, fairground; ice cream kiosks, snack bars, restaurants, pubs; toilets with ♿ ramps. *Dog restrictions:* from 1st April to 30th September dogs are restricted on various clearly marked areas of the beach.

• CENTRAL PROMENADE. Three-quarters of a mile long, sandy; naturally sheltered Promenade and good parking. *Safety and maintenance:* cleaned daily; Beach Safety Officers, warning signs. *Beach facilities:* deck chairs; donkeys, horses and carts, land train; ice cream kiosks, snack bars, pubs; toilets with ♿ ramps. *Dog restrictions:* from April 1st to 30th September dogs are restricted on various clearly marked areas of the beach.

FILEY

⚞ Family Fun Activities: Boating lake, putting, crazy golf, trampolines, children's play area, miniature golf • Folk Museum, Filey Dams Nature Reserve, Filey Brigg Nature Trail, Filey Sculpture Trail.

☆ Special Events: June/July: Filey Festival. July: Filey Regatta. August: Life Boat Day. August/September: Fishing Festival.

ⓘ **Tourist Information Centre, John Street, Filey YO14 9DW**
01723 383637 • Fax: 01723 518001
www.discoveryorkshirecoast.com

⚓ Beaches

• BEACH. Miles of open sand, naturally sheltered; parking. *Safety and maintenance:* cleaned daily, flagged, warning signs; lifeguards. *Beach facilities:* deckchairs, beach chalets; donkey rides; cafe and ice-cream kiosk; toilets with ⅊ access. *Dog restrictions:* banned between Coble Landing and Royal Parade (seasonal).

SCARBOROUGH

⚞ Family Fun Activities: Heated indoor pool, spa, sports centre, crown green bowls, 10-pin bowling, tennis, putting, two golf courses • Mini railway, boating lake, angling in harbour • Amusement arcades, bingo, cinemas, theatre, nightclubs • Museums and 12thC castle • Bird of Prey Centre, Shire Horse Farm, mini "naval warfare", Sea Life Centre, Honey Farm, Terror Tower, pleasure boat trips, Dino Days (Dinosaur Coast events).

ⓘ **Tourist Information Centre, Sandside, Scarborough YO11 1PP**
01723 383637 • Fax: 01723 383604
tourismbureau@scarborough.gov.uk
www.discoveryorkshirecoast.com

☆ Special Events: May/June: Scarborough Fayre; festivals, International Music Festival. July: Seafest. September: Jazz Festival.

⚓ Beaches

• NORTH BAY BEACH. Three-quarters of a mile long, sandy with rockpools and cliffs. Promenade, good parking. *Safety and maintenance:* cleaned daily; flagged, warning signs, lifeguards. *Beach facilities:* deck chairs and beach chalets; donkey rides; putting and boating lake. *Dog restrictions:* 1st May to 30th September - no dogs permitted between Scalby Mills and mini roundabout; must be kept on lead on Promenade.

• SOUTH BAY BEACH. Half a mile long, sandy and naturally sheltered. Promenade, bay includes Scarborough harbour with three piers. Good parking. *Safety and maintenance:* cleaned daily; flagged, warning signs, lifeguards. *Beach facilities:* deck chairs and beach chalets; donkey rides; swings and roundabouts; toilets with ⅊ access. *Dog restrictions:* 1st May to 30th September - no dogs permitted from West Pier to Spa Footbridge.

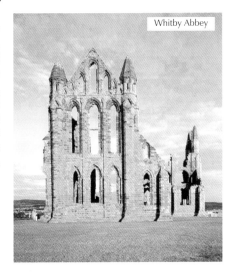
Whitby Abbey

WHITBY

Family Fun Activities: Heated indoor pool, boating, yachting, trout and salmon fishing, putting, crazy golf, golf,; bowls • Leisure Centre • Theatres, pavilion, museum, art gallery • Remains of 11th century abbey, Dracula Experience Trail, Captain Cook Heritage Trail, Funtastic indoor play area.

Special Events: March: Eskdale Festival of Arts. **August:** Whitby Regatta.

i **Tourist Information Centre,**
Langborne Road, Whitby YO21 1YN
01723 383637 • Fax: 01947 606137
tourismbureau@scarborough.gov.uk
www.discoveryorkshirecoast.com

Beaches

• BEACH. Three miles long, sandy and naturally sheltered. Good parking. *Safety and maintenance:* cleaned daily; warning signs, lifeguards. *Beach facilities:* deck chairs and beach chalets; donkey rides; ice cream kiosk and snack bar; toilets with & access. *Dog restrictions:* May to September – banned between Battery Parade and former Beach Cafe; must be kept on lead on Battery Parade and Promenade.

FREE AND REDUCED RATE HOLIDAY VISITS!
Don't miss our Readers' Offer Vouchers on pages 9-44

Fun for all the Family

COUNTY DURHAM

The Josephine and John Bowes Museum, Barnard Castle (01833 690606). Outstanding art collection, plus ceramics, porcelain, tapestries, and objects d'art (including Silver Swan automaton).
www.bowesmuseum.org.uk

Beamish, The North of England Open Air Museum, Beamish (0191 370 4000). A vivid re-creation of how people lived and worked at the turn of the century. Town Street, Home Farm, Colliery, Railway Station; tram rides, tea rooms.
www.beamish.org.uk

EAST YORKSHIRE

Elsham Hall Country and Wildlife Park, Near Brigg (01652 688698). See working craftsmen demonstrate their traditional skills in the craft centre set in beautiful grounds and lakeside gardens. Children's farm, lake, adventure playground, falconry centre.
www.elshamhall.co.uk

The Deep, Hull (01482 381000). Discover the story of the world's oceans on a dramatic journey back in time and into the future! The world's only underwater lift and Europe's deepest viewing tunnel!
www.thedeep.co.uk

NORTHUMBERLAND

Alnwick Castle (01665 510777). A mighty fortress, seat of the Duke of Northumberland since 1309. Location for the 'Harry Potter' films.
www.alnwickcastle.com

Grace Darling Museum, Bamburgh (01668 214465). Many original relics re-create the rescue by Grace and her father of the survivors of the wrecked Forfarshire.

Leaplish Waterside Park, Kielder Water (01434 220643). Ideal base for exploring the largest man-made lake in Britain; all sorts of sports, forest playground, restaurant.
www.kielder.org

☆ Fun for all the Family ☆

TEES VALLEY

◆ **Captain Cook Birthplace Museum, Middlesbrough (01642 311211).** Special effects add realism to the museum displays which tell the story of the famous explorer.

◆ **Hartlepool Historic Quay, Hartlepool (01429 860006).** Travel back in time to the sights, sounds and smells of 18th century seaport life. New attractions include children's adventure playship.
www.thisishartlepool.co.uk

◆ **Saltburn Smugglers Heritage Centre, Saltburn-by-the-Sea (01287 625252).** Experience the sights, sounds and smells of Saltburn's dark past in authentic settings.

TYNE & WEAR

◆ **Life Science Centre, Newcastle-upon-Tyne (0191 243 8223).** Discover just how truly amazing life is. Explore where life comes from and how it works. Meet your 4 billion year old family, find out what makes you unique, test your brainpower and enjoy the thrill of the Motion Simulator Ride.
www.lifesciencecentre.org.uk

◆ **Wildfowl and Wetlands Trust, Washington (0191-416 5454).** Have a great day out supporting conservation on a nose-to-beak voyage of discovery – many birds feed from the hand. Exhibition area, tea room, play area.
www.wwt.org.uk

NORTH & WEST YORKSHIRE

◆ **Colour Museum, Bradford (01274 390955).** Examines colour, light and the history of dyeing and textile printing. Interactive galleries and workshops.
www.sdc.org.uk/museum

◆ **Eden Camp Modern History Theme Museum, Malton (01653 697777).** Civilian life in Britain during WWII – experience the sights, sounds and even smells of 1939-1945 at this award-winning museum.
www.edencamp.co.uk

◆ **Flamingo Land Theme Park, Zoo and Holiday Village, off Malton-Pickering Road (0870 7528000).** Rides and slides, zoo, indoor playcentre, cable car ride etc.
www.flamingoland.co.uk

◆ **Lightwater Valley Theme Park, Ripon (0870 458 0040).** The world's longest roller coaster, thrill rides, theatre, crazy golf, boating lake and much more. Restaurant and cafes.
www.lightwatervalley.co.uk

◆ **National Museum of Photography, Film and Television, Bradford (0870 701 0200).** Packed with things to do and find out, this bright, modern museum is a fun day out for all the family, telling the fascinating story of still and moving pictures.
www.nmpft.org.uk

◆ **National Railway Museum, York (01904 621261).** See how Britain's railways shaped the world at the largest railway museum in the world. BR's up to-the-minute exhibit gives a glimpse into the future. Restaurant and gift shop.
www.nrm.org.uk

◆ **Royal Armouries Museum, Leeds (0113-220 1916).** New attraction with thousands of items from a collection previously housed in the Tower of London. Jousting displays, Wild West gun fights, Oriental swordsmanship, plus lots more.
www.armouries.org.uk

NORTH WEST ENGLAND

Best Beaches

There are lovely stretches of coastline and clean sands, and lively resorts whose efforts to maintain their high place in British holiday planning are showing successful results - Blackpool South Beach and St Annes Pier have earned a Quality Coast Award.

i North West Tourism
(Cheshire, Greater Manchester, High Peak, Lancashire, Merseyside).

• e-mail: venw@nwda.cco.uk
• www.englandsnorthwest.com

Blackpool and the Tower

For more information about holidaying in the North West see:
•www.visitlancashire.com
•www.visitchester.com
•www.golakes.co.uk
•www.visitliverpool.com
•www.visitmanchester.com

BLACKPOOL

Family Fun Activities: Pleasure Beach with over 145 rides and attractions including Europe's tallest, fastest roller-coaster and Valhalla, the world's biggest dark ride • Blackpool Tower with 7 levels of fun including a circus, ballroom, adventure playground and aquarium • Zoo, Sealife Centre, Sandcastle Waterworld indoor water paradise, Louis Tussaud's Waxworks • Stanley Park with lake, Italian Gardens, bowling, children's playgrounds, putting and Sports Centre • Three piers with arcades, shows and amusements, Winter Gardens with ballroom and Opera House, Grand Theatre • 10-pin bowling, golf, putting, go-karts, fishing, swimming pools • Multiplex cinemas, shows, pubs.

Special Events: July/August: Kids MegaFest Children's Festival. **1st September to 5th November:** Blackpool Illuminations.

i **Blackpool Tourism, 1 Clifton Street, Blackpool FYl lLY • 01253 478222 e-mail: tourism@blackpool.gov.uk www.visitblackpool.com**

Beaches

• BEACH. Approximately 7 miles long, sandy. Promenade, tramcars; good parking. *Safety and maintenance:* foreshore flagged, warning signs; lifeguards; beach cleaned daily. *Beach facilities:* deck chairs, donkey rides; ice cream kiosks, snack bars, restaurants, pubs; toilets with special needs access and mother/baby changing facilities. *Dog restrictions:* banned from the beach between North Pier and South Pier from May to September; must be kept on a lead on every street in Blackpool.

LYTHAM ST ANNES

Family Fun Activities: Heated indoor pool; pier, donkey rides on beach; children's playground, boating lake, floral gardens; tennis, putting, bowls, trampolines; miniature railway; golf courses (4); sailing; pubs, cafes and restaurants; theatre at Lytham; RSPB Discovery Centre at Fairhaven Lake.

Special Events: May/August: Carnivals and Fete days, miscellaneous local shows and competitions throughout the year.

i **Visitor and Travel Information, Lytham St Annes FY8 ILH 01253 725610 • Fax: 01253 640708**

Beaches

• BEACH. Sandy, three miles long, and backed by dunes and promenade. Pier with arcade and refreshments. Good parking. *Safety and maintenance:* patches of soft sand and mud; river estuary; warning signs. Cleaned daily in season. *Beach facilities:* deck chairs, donkey rides; ice cream kiosks, snack bars, restaurants; toilets with ♿ access. *Dog restrictions:* can be exercised north of St. Annes pier, past the high water mark.

MORECAMBE

⚒ Family Fun Activities: Superbowl, cinema, Megazone, Happy Mount Park • Promenade and play areas, Stone Jetty with seabird-themed pavement games, the Eric Morecambe Stage and Statue Arcades and amusements..

☆ Special Events: September: Golf Festival, Heritage Open Days, Heritage Gala.

[ℹ] **Morecambe Tourist Information Centre, Old Station Buildings, Marine Road Central, Morecambe LA4 4DB 01524 582808 • Fax: 01524 832549 e-mail: morecambetic@lancaster.gov.uk www.citycoastcountryside.co.uk**

⛱ Beaches

• BEACH. Several stretches of sand, backed by 5 mile long flat promenade with beautiful views across the wide expanse of Morecambe Bay towards the Lake District. Ample parking. *Safety and maintenance:* safety signs and lifebelts; Promenade Supervisor. *Beach facilities:* ice cream kiosks; toilets incl. some with ♿ access; miniature train. *Dog restrictions:* dogs not allowed on amenity beaches.

☆ Fun for all the Family ☆

CHESHIRE

◆ **Blue Planet Aquarium, Ellesmere Port (0151 357 8804).** The UK's largest aquarium with moving walkway through tropical fish and a large collection of sharks. **www.blueplanetaquarium.com**

◆ **Boat Museum, Ellesmere Port (0151-355 5017).** World's largest floating collection of canal craft on a 7-acre site. Steam engines, blacksmith's forge etc. Cafe. **www.boatmuseum.org.uk**

◆ **Brookside Miniature Railway, Poynton (01625 872919).** Cheshire's greatest little railway. Super train rides, authentic detail in half-mile circuit of gardens. Restaurant. **www.brookside-miniature.railway.co.uk**

◆ **Catalyst, Widnes (0151-420 1121).** Science and technology comes alive with hands-on exhibits, observatory. The only science centre solely devoted to chemistry, with over 30 interactive exhibits. **www.catalyst.org.uk**

◆ **Chester Zoo, Chester (01244 380280).** Britain's largest zoo outside London. Spacious enclosures. Restaurants and cafeteria. **www.chesterzoo.org.uk**

◆ **Jodrell Bank Science Centre, Planetarium and Arboretum, Near Macclesfield (01477 571339).** 'Hands on' gallery and space exhibition; planetarium. Lovell Radio Telescope. **www.jb.man.ac.uk**

☆ Fun for all the Family ☆

CUMBRIA

◆ **Cars of the Stars Motor Museum, Keswick (017687 73757).** Celebrity TV and film vehicles including Chitty Chitty Bang Bang and the Batmobile plus film set displays.
www.carsofthestars.com

◆ **The Cumberland Pencil Museum, Southey Works, Keswick (017687 73626).** The first-ever pencils were produced in Keswick and the museum traces the history of this everyday writing instrument. See the longest pencil in the world.
www.pencils.co.uk

◆ **Eden Ostrich World, Penrith (01768 881771).** See these magnificent birds in the setting of a real farm on the banks of the River Eden. Play areas, farm animals.
www.ostrich-world.com

◆ **Lake District National Park Visitor Centre, Brockhole, Windermere (01539 724555).** Exciting Lake District exhibitions, including the 'Living Lakeland' display. Restaurant and tearooms.
www.lake-district.gov.uk

◆ **Rheged, The Upland Kingdom Discovery Centre. Penrith (01768 868000).** Journey through 2000 years of Cumbria's magic in this new attraction set under a grass-covered roof. Discover the village in the hill.
www.rheged.com

◆ **Windermere Steamboat Museum, Windermere (015394 45565).** A unique collection of Victorian steam launches and other historic craft. Steam launch trips subject to weather and availability.
www.steamboat.co.uk

GREATER MANCHESTER

◆ **The Lowry, Salford (0870 787 5780).** A world-class venue for performing and visual arts. Theatres and galleries.
www.thelowry.com

◆ **Museum of Science and Industry, Manchester (0161-832 2244).** Like no other museum you've ever been in. Xperiment! – interactive science centre; Power Hall; Victorian Sewers – and lots more.
www.msim.org.uk

LANCASHIRE

◆ **Blackpool Tower (01253 292029).** 520 ft high, houses a circus, aquarium, dance hall and other shows. The famous Illuminations start early in September.
www.theblackpooltower.co.uk

◆ **Wildfowl Trust, Martin Mere (01704 895181).** Exotic and native breeds plus thousands of migrant visitors observed from spacious hides.
www.wwt.org.uk

MERSEYSIDE

◆ **The Beatles Story, Liverpool (0151-709 1963).** Re-live the sights and sounds of the Swinging Sixties a magical mystery tour!
www.beatlesstory.com

◆ **World of Glass, St Helens (08707 114466).** The fascinating history of glass-making. Enter the magical mirror maze and explore the cone building tunnels.
www.worldofglass.com

SCOTLAND

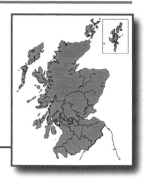

Best Beaches

Scotland has a huge coastline, one of the longest in Europe, with great stretches of sand along the Solway, on the Ayrshire coast, East Lothian and Fife, around Aberdeen, along the Moray Firth and in the North West. Good beach management practices have been rewarded with five European Blue Flags. In addition Seaside Awards (Resort and Rural Categories) have gone to 51 beaches which meet the high standards required.

BLUE FLAG BEACHES 2007
- *St Andrews West Sands*
- *Elie Harbour*
- *Aberdour Silver Sands*
- *Burntisland*
- *Montrose*

[i] Scottish Tourist Board
- Tel: 0845 2255 121
- e-mail: info@visitscotland.com
- www.visitscotland.com

ABERDEEN

⛫ Family Fun Activities: Winter Gardens, Art Gallery, museums, cinemas, theatres, Music Hall • Doonies Farm, Hazlehead Park, Aberdeen Fun Beach, Satrosphere Hands-on Science Centre, Storybook Glen • Windsurfing, bowling, squash, tennis, Linx Ice Arena, cricket, rugby, riding, walking, climbing, fishing, golf.

[i] **Aberdeen Visitor Information Centre, 23 Union Street, Aberdeen AB11 5BP 01224 288828 e-mail: Aberdeen@visitscotland.com www.aberdeen-grampian.com**

⛱ Beaches

• BEACH. Two and a half miles of sandy beach, promenade and harbour; ample parking. *Safety and maintenance:* cleaned daily; lifeboats, lifebelts; lifeguards in summer. Aberdeen Fun Beach: Scotland's largest family entertainment centre, open all year. Restaurants, multi-plex cinema, leisure centre with swimming pool and flumes, ice arena, indoor and outdoor funfair, ten-pin bowling, pool and Ramboland – children's adventure play area

ISLE OF ARRAN

⛫ Family Fun Activities: This peaceful island, "Scotland in Miniature", offers a wealth of leisure activities and places of interest including Brodick Castle, Gardens and Country Park, Isle of Arran Distillery, Balmichael Visitor Centre, Isle of Arran Heritage Museum, Arran Aromatics.

[i] **Tourist Information Centre, The Pier, Brodick KA27 8AU 0845 2255 121 e-mail: Brodick@visitscotland.com www.ayrshire-arran.com**

☆ **Special Events:** **July:** Arran Fleadh. **August:** Highland Games. **October:** Ladies Golf Competition. **November:** Gents Golf Competition.

⛱ Beaches

• BEACHES. Varied coastline with shingle and pebble shores and sandy beaches suitable for all the family.

AYR

⛫ Family Fun Activities: Citadel Leisure Complex • Swimming pool, 10-pin bowling, golf, putting, pitch and putt, cricket, tennis, bowls • Cinema, dancing/discos • Racecourse • Nearby Burns National Heritage Park, Belleisle Park, Rozelle Park, Craig Tara, Heads of Ayr Park.

☆ **Special Events:** **May:** Ayr Agricultural Show. **June:** Ayr Golf Week. **August:** Flower Show. **September:** Ayr Gold Cup (horse racing).

[i] **Tourist Information Centre, 22 Sandgate, Ayr KA7 1BW 0845 2255 121 e-mail: Ayr@visitscotland.com www.ayrshire-arran.com**

⛱ Beaches

• BEACH. Two and a half miles long, sand and some shingle; promenade and harbour; ample parking. *Beach facilities:* children's playground, crazy golf, boating pond, putting on promenade; cafes; toilets with ♿ access.

GIRVAN

Family Fun Activities: Swimming pool, golf, putting, tennis, bowls • Boat trips and fishing.

Special Events: **May:** Folk Festival. **June:** Civic Week. **August:** Annual Maidens Harbour Gala. **October:** Folk Festival.

Beaches

• BEACH. One and a half miles long, sandy and some shingle; promenade and harbour, ample parking. *Beach facilities:* children's playground, boating pond; toilets with &. access.

LARGS

Family Fun Activities: Swimming pool, sauna/solarium; tennis, putting, squash, golf, bowling, windsurfing, diving. • Vikingar, Kelburn Castle & Country Centre

Special Events: **August:** Regatta Week. **September:** Viking Festival.

i Tourist Information Centre,
The Station, Largs
0845 2255 121
e-mail: Largs@visitscotland.com
www.ayrshire-arran.com

Beaches

• BEACH. Shingle and sand; promenade, parking; boating pond; cafes and ice cream kiosks; toilets with &. access.

MILLPORT

Family Fun Activities: Organised children's activities • Tennis, pitch and putt, trampolines, golf, riding, cycle hire, bowling, fun fair • Museum, aquarium at Marine Station • The Cathedral of the Isles (smallest cathedral in Britain). Millport is reached by car/passenger ferry from Largs; 10 minute bus ride from ferry slip to town.

Special Events: **July/August:** Country and Western Festival, Cumbrae Weekend.

Beaches

• BEACH. Sand and shingle, rock pools; parking. *Beach facilities:* cafes and shops nearby, toilets, some with &. access. *Dog restrictions:* must be kept on lead.

TROON

Family Fun Activities: golf, bowling, tennis, swimming, children's play areas.

Special Events: **June:** Gala Week.

i www.ayrshire-arran.com

Beaches

• BEACH. Excellent sandy beach with first-aid and life saving equipment nearby. Toilets.

Looking for holiday accommodation?
search for details of properties where children are welcome
www.holidayguides.com

ROTHESAY

⚓ **Family Fun Activities:** Main town on the Isle of Bute easily reached by car/passenger ferry from Wemyss Bay or Colintraive • Pavilion with family variety shows, children's entertainment • Mount Stuart, Isle of Bute Discovery Centre and cinema/theatre, Rothesay Castle, Bute Museum • Putting, tennis, bowling, golf, pony trekking • Leisure Pool with sauna/solarium • Ornamental gardens, castle and museum, walks.

i Isle of Bute Discovery Centre,
**Victoria Street, Rothesay,
Isle of Bute PA20 0AH
0845 2255 121
e-mail: Rothesay@visitscotland.com
www.VisitBute.com**

ST ANDREWS

⚓ **Family Fun Activities:** Historic University town with 13th century Castle and 12th century Cathedral, St Andrews Museum, St Andrews Aquarium, Craigtoun Country Park, East Sands Leisure Centre • Bowling, tennis, putting, and (of course) GOLF (British Golf Museum) • Theatre, cinema, arts centre. • Fun town tours, sandcastle building competitions (summer months).

i Tourist Information Centre,
**70 Market Street, St Andrews KY16 9NU
01334 472021
e-mail: Standrews@visitscotland.com
www.visitfife.com**

🏖 Beaches

• **WEST SANDS.** Wide, flat sandy beach. Within walking distance of town centre, ample parking. *Safety and maintenance:* cleaned regularly and patrolled by council staff. *Beach facilities:* catering outlets; toilets. *Dog restrictions:* banned from most of beach in summer months.

• **EAST SANDS.** Sandy beach, just past the harbour; parking. *Safety and maintenance:* cleaned regularly. *Beach facilities:* catering facilities; watersports; toilets. *Dog restrictions:* none.

Galloway Wildlife Conservation Park, near Kirkcudbright

See Readers' Offer Voucher

☆ Fun for all the Family ☆

NORTHERN SCOTLAND

Anderson's Storybook Glen, Maryculter, near Aberdeen (01224 732941). Old Woman's Shoe, Pixie Park, Old MacDonald, play park and the Three Bears' House. Waterfalls.

Archaeolink Prehistory Park, near Insch (01464 851500). All-weather attraction with events inside and out, exhibition and film theatre, all set in 40 acres. www.archaeolink.co.uk

Cawdor Castle, Nairn (01667 404401). A 14th century Keep, fortified in the 15th century and the 17th century, the massive fortress is set in splendid grounds with nature trails and gardens. Shops, snack bar, picnic area, restaurant and golf course. www.cawdorcastle.com

Buckie Drifter Maritime Heritage Centre, Buckie (01542 8346460. See how the herring industry worked in the past and walk along a re-created 1920's quayside. www.moray.org/bdrifter

Eilean Donan Castle, near Kyle of Lochalsh (01599 555202). Probably the most photographed castle in Scotland, Eilean Donan stands in a romantic and picturesque setting on Loch Duich. www.eieandonancastle.com

Glamis Castle, near Forfar(01307 840393). Childhood home of the Queen Mother and birthplace of Princess Margaret. Visitors have a choice of admission to the Castle/grounds/formal garden/coach house /nature trail/picnic areas, including a children's play area. www.strathmore-estates.co.uk

Highland Mysteryworld, Glencoe (01855 811660). Five fabulous indoor attractions in spectacular setting at foot of Glencoe. Also adventure playground and leisure centre

Highland Wildlife Park, Kincraig (01540 651270). Over 250 acres with red deer, European bison, wild horses, roe deer, Soay sheep, Highland cattle, wandering freely amidst magnificent Highland scenery. www.highlandwildlifepark.org

Kylerhea Otter Haven, Kylerhea, Isle of Skye (01320 366322). See otters in their natural habitat and view other wildlife from a spacious hide.

Landmark Visitor Centre, Carrbridge (01479 841613). Attractions include tree-top trail, pine forest nature centre, woodland maze and adventure playground with giant slide and aerial walkways. www.landmark-centre.co.uk

The Official Loch Ness Monster Exhibition Centre, Drumnadrochit (01456 450573). Explore the mysteries surrounding the existence (or not!) of Nessie, the world-famous monster. www.loch-ness-scotland.com

Timespan Heritage Centre, Helmsdale (01431 821327). Award-winning heritage centre telling the dramatic story of the Highlands. Landscaped garden with collection of rare herbal medicinal plants. www.timespan.org.uk

☆ Fun for all the Family ☆

CENTRAL SCOTLAND

◆ **Bannockburn Heritage Centre, near Stirling (01786 812664).** Superb audio visual presentation and magnificent equestrian statue of Robert the Bruce.
www.nts.org.uk/bannockburn

◆ **Blair Drummond Safari & Adventure Park (01786 841456).** Drive through animal reserves, monkey jungle. Pets farm – even a boat safari round chimp island – plus rides, amusements .
www.safari-park.co.uk

◆ **British Golf Museum, St Andrews (01334 460046).** Relive all the history and atmosphere of 500 years of golf. Themed galleries feature the tournaments, players and equipment which today's game.
www.britishgolfmuseum.co.uk

◆ **Deep Sea World, North Queensferry (01383 411880).** An underwater safari beneath the Firth of Forth gives a superb view of thousands of fish as they travel along the longest underwater tunnel in the world.
www.deepseaworld.com

◆ **Falkirk Wheel (08700 500208).** A mechanical marvel, the world's only rotating boatlift used to connect the Forth & Clyde and Union canals.
www.thefalkirkwheel.co.uk

◆ **Frigate Unicorn, Victoria Dock, Dundee (01382 200900).** An 1824 wooden, 46 gun frigate; Britain's oldest ship afloat restored as a floating museum.
www.frigateunicorn.org

◆ **Museum of Transport, Kelvin Hall, Glasgow (0141-287 2720).** The oldest cycle in the world, trams, bikes, trains, horse drawn vehicles, special displays, models and more.
www.seeglasgow.com

◆ **New Lanark, Near Lanark (01555 661345).** An insight into the lives of working men and women in this restored conservation village in an attractive situation by the Falls of Clyde. A World Heritage site.
www.newlanark.org

◆ **Our Dynamic Earth, Edinburgh (0131 550 7800).** Charting the Earth's development over the last 4,500 million years with lots of interactive entertainment for adults and children.
www.dynamicearth.co. uk

◆ **St Andrews Sea Life Aquarium (01334 474786).** Hundreds of different species in displays intended to re-create their natural habitat. Includes playful seals and colourful tropical fish.
www.standrewsaquarium.co.uk

◆ **Scottish Fisheries Museum, Anstruther (01333 310628).** A unique record of Scotland's fishing industry. Museum shop and tearoom. Restored fisherman's cottage.
www.scottish-fisheries-museum.org

◆ **Scottish Deer Centre, Over Rankeilour Farm, near Cupar(01337 810391).** Audio visual show. Outdoor and indoor play areas and the chance to study (and stroke) these beautiful animals at close quarters.

☆ Fun for all the Family ☆

SOUTHERN SCOTLAND

◆ **Brodick Castle and Country Park (01770 302202).** Former seat of the Dukes of Hamilton (now NT) with fine examples of silver, porcelain and paintings. Woodland walks, formal garden; ranger service. **www.nts.org.uk/brodick**

◆ **Burns National Heritage Park, Alloway (01292 443700).** Burns Cottage Museum, Auld Kirk, Tam O' Shanter Experience, Brig O' Doon, Burns Monument and Gardens — all within half a mile of each other. **www.burnsheritagepark.com**

◆ **Culzean Castle and Country Park, By Maybole (01655 884455).** Castle designed by Robert Adam in 1777; park with deer, swans, walled garden, aviary, restaurant and tearoom. **www.nts.org.uk/culzean**

◆ **Floors Castle, Kelso (01573 223333).** Scotland's largest inhabited castle with magnificent collections of tapestries, furniture and porcelain. Gift shop and restaurant. **www.floorscastle.com**

◆ **Harestanes Countryside Visitor Centre, Jedburgh (01835 830306).** Wildlife garden and temporary exhibitions. Games and puzzles, adventure play area, tearoom, gift shop. Woodland walks.

◆ **Kelburn Castle & Country Centre, Fairlie (01475 568204).** Historic home of the Earls of Glasgow, with beautiful garden walks, tea room, pony trekking, adventure course, children's stockade, pets' corner and The Secret Forest. **www.kelburnecastle.com**

◆ **Loudoun Castle Park, Galston (01563 822296).** Fun for all the family, with amusements and rides (including Britain's largest carousel), castle ruin, animals, aviary, restaurant and gift shop. **www.loudouncastle.co.uk**

◆ **Magnum Leisure Centre, Irvine (01294 278381).** Swimming pool complex, ice rink, sports hall, bowls hall, fitness suite, fast food outlet, theatre/cinema and soft play area. **www.themagnum.co.uk**

◆ **Traquair House, Near Innerleithen (01896 830323).** Oldest inhabited historic mansion in Scotland. Treasures date from 12th century, unique secret staircase to Priest's Room, craft workshop, woodland walks, maze, brewery.

◆ **Thirlestane Castle, Lauder (01578 722430).** Border country life exhibitions in magnificent castle. Historic toys, woodland walk and picnic areas. Tearoom and gift shop. **www.thirlestanecastle.co.uk**

◆ **Vikingar! Largs (01475 689777).** Let live Viking guides take you on an enthralling multi-media journey back in time to trace the history of the Vikings in Scotland. Also swimming pool, soft play area, cinema/theatre and cafe/bar. **www.vikingar.co.uk**

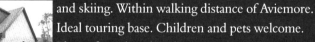

FHG Guides

**publish a large range of well-known accommodation guides.
We will be happy to send you details or you can use
the order form at the back of this book.**

SPEYSIDE LEISURE PARK

Self-Catering Holidays in the Heart of the Highlands

The park is situated in a quiet riverside setting with mountain views, only a short walk from Aviemore centre and shops. We offer a range of warm, well equipped chalets, cabins and caravans, including a caravan for the disabled. Prices include electricity, gas, linen, towels and use of our heated indoor pool and sauna. There are swings, a climbing frame and low level balance beams for the children. Permit fishing is available on the river. Discounts are given on some local attractions.

Families, couples or groups will find this an ideal location for a wide range of activities including:

• *Horse riding* • *Golf* • *Fishing* • *Hillwalking*
• *RSPB Reserves* • *Mountain and Watersports* • *Reindeer herd*
• *Steam railway and the Whisky Trail*

Only slightly further afield you will find Culloden Moor, the Moray Firth dolphins and of course, the not to be missed, Loch Ness.
Accommodation sleeps from 4-8, but we offer a reduced rate for a couple. Short Breaks are available. Sorry, no pets, except guide and hearing dogs.

Speyside Leisure Park
Dalfaber Road, Aviemore, Inverness-shire PH22 1PX
Tel: 01479 810236 • Fax: 01479 811688
e-mail: fhg@speysideleisure.com • www.speysideleisure.com

COLOGIN – a haven in the hills

If you've just got married or just retired, have toddlers in tow or dogs you can't bear to leave at home, or you just want to get away for a break with all the freedom of a self-catering holiday, then we may have just what you are looking for. Our cosy chalets and well appointed lodges offer everything you need for a relaxing country holiday.

One of the most appealing features of Cologin is its peace and tranquillity. With 14 lodges, 4 chalets and Cruachan Cottage at Cologin we have plenty of different accommodation options. Choose from a cosy one-bedroom chalet or the larger two-bedroomed lodges, including: pet-free, pet-friendly, wheelchair accessible and non-smoking.

Our award-winning family-friendly pub and restaurant, *The Barn,* is within easy reach of all our properties. It's a perfect place to unwind and relax. With its unique atmosphere and friendly staff it is the reason why many of Cologin's guests return year after year.

If you love the great outdoors come rain or shine and want to escape from the routine of city life, Cologin is for you. With 17,000 acres of waymarked forest trails above the farm you can enjoy nature at its finest, with glorious scenery and breathtaking views from the summit over Oban Bay to the islands beyond.

Contact us for colour brochure:
Jim and Linda Battison – resident owners
Cologin, Lerags Glen, Oban, Argyll PA34 4SE
Telephone: 01631 564501 • Fax: 01631 566925
e-mail: info@cologin.co.uk
www.cologin.co.uk

COLOGIN
a haven in the hills
STB ★★★–★★★★
Self Catering

WALES

 Best Beaches

A grand total of 39 resort beaches in Wales have been awarded the European Blue Flag for 2007, and an impressive number have received Seaside Awards (Resort and Rural Categories). Seaside Awards are given to well-managed beaches which comply with the legal minimum microbiological standards of water quality.

BLUE FLAG BEACHES 2007

- *Anglesey*
  Benllech, Llanddona, Llanddwyn, Porth Dafarch, Trearddur Bay
- *Gwynedd*
  Barmouth (Abermaw),
Abersoch, Pwllheli, Fairbourne, Dinas Dinlle, Tywyn
- *North Wales*
  Llandudno (North Shore), Llandudno (West Shore), Penmaenmawr, Prestatyn
- *Carmarthenshire*
  Pembrey Country Park, Pendine
- *Ceredigion*
  Aberystwyth (North), Aberystwyth (South),
  New Quay (Harbour), Borth, Tresaith

- *Pembrokeshire*
  Broadhaven (North), Dale, Saundersfoot, Lydstep, Tenby (Castle), Tenby (South), Tenby (North), St Davids (Whitesands), Poppit Sands, Newgale
- *South Wales*
  Porthcawl (Rest Bay), Bracelet Bay, Caswell Bay, Port Eynon, Langland Bay, Trecco Bay, Barry (Whitmore Bay)

 VisitWales
- Tel: 08708 300306
- Fax: 08701 211259
- e-mail: info@visitwales.com
- www.visitwales.co.uk

ABERYSTWYTH

⚓ **Family Fun Activities:** Sports and leisure centre, swimming pools, children's playgrounds, parks, promenade, outdoor paddling pool • Narrow gauge railway, electric cliff railway, camera obscura, marina, castle, hill fort, National Library of Wales, theatre, cinema • Nature reserves and forestry centres, farm park, boat trips, coastal paths, cycle path.

ℹ️ **Tourist Information Centre, Terrace Road, Aberystwyth SY23 2AG
01970 612125 • Fax: 01970 626566
aberystwythtic@ceredigion.gov.uk
www.tourism.ceredigion.gov.uk**

🏖️ **Beaches**

• BEACH. Two-award-winning sloping beaches of coarse grey sand and shingle; North Beach fronted by promenade, parking on sea front; South Beach has ample parking. *Safety and maintenance:* water quality on both beaches usually good. Beach Officer/lifeguard usually on duty July/August. *Beach facilities:* rock pools, donkey rides; paddling pool etc on promenade; restaurants and kiosks; toilets. *Dog restrictions:* dogs banned between 1st May and 30th September on North Beach between jetty and Constitution Hill, and on South Beach between Castle headland and first groyne on South Marine Terrace

COLWYN BAY

⚓ **Family Fun Activities:** Welsh Mountain Zoo, Eirias Park with leisure centre, swimming pool, picnic and play areas, boating lake, model yacht pond, indoor tennis centre and skateboarding area • Pier and promenade with cycle track, Puppet Theatre, cricket ground and children's outdoor paddling pool at Rhos-on-Sea • Angling, bowling, golf, walking, watersports • Theatre/cinema with shows all year round.

⭐ **Special Events:** **May Bank Holiday:** Bay of Colwyn Promenade Day. **August:** Festive Fridays - every Friday in August.

ℹ️ **Information Centre, Imperial Buildings, Princes Drive, Colwyn Bay
01492 530478
e-mail: colwynbay@nwtic.com
www.colwyn-bay-tourism.co.uk**

🏖️ **Beaches**

• BEACH. Sandy beach with easy access along A55 expressway. *Beach facilities:* kiosks; ♿ toilets operate on National Key system.

**FREE AND REDUCED RATE
HOLIDAY VISITS!**
Don't miss our **Readers'
Offer Vouchers**
on pages 9-44

FHG Guides
publish a large range of well-known accommodation guides.
We will be happy to send you details or you can use
the order form at the back of this book.

LLANDUDNO

Family Fun Activities: Pier • putting, paddling pool, indoor swimming pool, yacht pond • Alice in Wonderland memorial on West Shore promenade, tramway and cable car to Great Orme Country Park and Visitor Centre, Great Orme Copper Mines, boat trips, Punch & Judy, 10-pin bowling • Llandudno Museum, Alice in Wonderland Visitor Centre, Bodafon Farm Park, Ski & Snowboard Centre with toboggan run • Theatre, art gallery • Victorian shopping centre.

Special Events: **May Bank Holiday:** Victorian Extravaganza. **June:** Gwyl Llandudno Festival - a summer arts festival. **July:** vehicle rally; Fun day, Bodafon Fields; various promenade events. **November:** Celtic Winter Fayre.

[i] **Tourist Information Centre, Chapel Street, Llandudno LL30 2UY 01492 876413 e-mail: llandudnotic@conwy.gov.uk www.llandudno-tourism.co.uk**

Beaches

• NORTH SHORE BEACH. Two miles long, sand and shingle, naturally sheltered; promenade and pier with amusements etc. *Safety and maintenance:* safe bathing beach. *Beach facilities:* deck chairs, donkey rides; pub and hotels on promenade; ice cream kiosks, snack bars etc nearby; toilets with & access at eastern end.

• WEST SHORE BEACH. Sandy beach, one mile long; promenade and parking. *Safety and maintenance:* warning signs (sand banks can be dangerous on incoming tide). *Beach facilities:* children's play area; snack bar.

PORTHCAWL

Family Fun Activities: A variety of activities ranging from sports to all the fun of the fair.

Special Events: **February:** Celtic Festival of Wales. **April:** Porthcawl Jazz Festival. **July/August:** Porthcawl Town Carnival; Sea Festival. **September:** Elvis Festival.

[i] **Heritage Coast Tourist Information Centre, Old Police Station, John Street, Porthcawl CF36 3DT • 01656 786639 e-mail: porthcawltic@bridgend.gov.uk www.visitbridgend.com**

Beaches

• BEACHES. Trecco Bay and Rest Bay offer miles of golden sands; parking and good disabled access. *Beach facilities:* deckchairs; cafes and ice-cream kiosks; toilets nearby in town. *Dog restrictions:* banned in summer from June onwards.

TENBY

Family Fun Activities: Safe, sandy beaches • Leisure centre, amusement arcade, bowls, putting, sailing, pony trekking, golf courses• Pavilion (plays, variety shows, dancing, concerts etc), male voice choir concerts • Museum and art gallery, 15th century Tudor Merchant's House, aquarium, art galleries • The town is pedestrianised during July and August.

Special Events: Air Sea Rescue and Helicopter Displays; Winter and Summer Carnivals, brass bands, Arts Festival.

[i] **Information Centre, Tenby 01834 842402 tenby.tic@pembrokeshire.gov.uk**

☆ Fun for all the Family ☆

NORTH WALES

◆ **Alice in Wonderland Centre, Llandudno (01492 860082).** Pop down the rabbit hole and see the Alice story come to life in colourful scenes. Souvenir shop. A must for all Lewis Carroll fans.
www.wonderland.co.uk

◆ **Anglesey Sea Zoo, Brynsiencyn (01248 430411).** Meet the fascinating creatures that inhabit the seas and shores around Anglesey; adventure playground, children's activities, shops and restaurants.
www.angleseyseazoo.co.uk

◆ **Bodafon Farm Park, Llandudno (01492 549060).** Enjoy a tractor/trailer ride around the paddocks and see the variety of rare breed animals, including shire horses, llamas, and peacocks. Shop, cafe and adventure playground.
www.bodafon.co.uk

◆ **Electric Mountain Visitor Centre, Llanberis (01286 870636).** Discover the amazing powers of hydro-electricity in an exciting and interactive environment.
www.electricmountain.co.uk

◆ **Henblas Park, Bodorgan (01407 840440).** Situated in the heart of Anglesey, with lots to see and do - shearing demonstrations, duck display, indoor adventure playground, farm animals - entertainment for the whole family, whatever the weather.
www.parc-henblas-park.co.uk

◆ **Knights Cavern, Rhyl (01745 338562).** Spine chilling walk through supernatural, mythological Wales. "Tortures in the Castle" is guaranteed to shiver your timbers!

◆ **Museum of Childhood Memories, Beaumaris (01248 712498).** Over 2000 items in themed rooms will delight and fascinate all ages – from teddy bears to clockwork trains.

◆ **Pili Palas, Anglesey (01248 712474).** Exotic butterflies and birds in natural settings, plus (the children's favourites!) creepy crawlies and reptiles. Picnic area, cafe and adventure playground.
www.pilipalas.co.uk

◆ **Sea Life Centre, Rhyl (01745 344660).** Spectacular underwater tunnel allows you to walk through sharks, stingrays and other sea creatures. Regular talks, feeding displays and demonstrations; gift shop.
www.rhyl.com/sealife

◆ **Snowdon Mountain Railway, Llanberis (0870 458 0033).** Travel by train on Britain's only rack and pinion railway up Snowdon. the highest mountain in England and Wales. A masterpiece of Victorian engineeering.
www.snowdonrailway.co.uk

◆ **Sygun Copper Mine, Beddgelert (01766 890595).** Stalagmites and stalactites formed from ferrous oxide. Award-winning attraction with underground audio visual tours.
www.syguncoppermine.co.uk

◆ **Welsh Mountain Zoo, Colwyn Bay (01492 532938).** Magnificent animals in natural surroundings, plus Chimpanzee World, Jungle Adventureland and Tarzan Trail, children's farm, etc - a great day out.
www.welshmountainzoo.org

☆ Fun for all the Family ☆

MID WALES

◆ **Borth Animalarium, Borth (01970 871224).** Domestic and farm animals in the petting barn; exoic and endangered species in large enclosures. Pony rides and handling sessions. Indoor and outdoor play areas; cafe and shop
www.animalarium.co.uk

◆ **Centre for Alternative Technology, Machynlleth (01654 705950).** A "green" village with displays of sustainable and renewable sources of power eg solar, wind. Energy saving houses, organic gardens, bookshop. Adventure playground, restaurant.

www.cat.org.uk

◆ **Chwarel Hen Slate Caverns, Llanfair, Near Harlech (01766 780247).** Self-guided tours of awesome series of slate caverns – spooky in places, but memorable. Also children's farmyard.

◆ **Felinwynt Rainforest and Butterfly Centre, Rhosmaen, Near Aberporth (01239 810882).** Exotic butterflies flying freely in a hothouse atmosphere amid tropical plants and the taped sounds of a Peruvian rainforest.
www.felinwyntrainforest.co.uk

◆ **King Arthur's Labyrinth, Machynlleth (01654 761584).** Sail along an underground river into a world of mystery, legends and storytelling. Also Bards' Quest maze and Corris Craft Centre with many original crafts and workshops. Cafe, outdoor play area.
www.kingarthurslabyrinth.co.uk

◆ **Llywernog Silver-Lead Mine, Ponterwyd, Aberystwyth (01970 890620).** Underground tours and miners' trail telling the story of the hunt for gold and silver in the Welsh hills.
www.silverminetours.co.uk

◆ **Portmeirion Italianate Village, Near Penrhyndeudraeth (01766 770000).** The most "un-Welsh" village in Wales, with the atmosphere of a strange, self-contained world. Location of 'The Prisoner' TV series in the mid-60s.
www.portmeirion.wales.com

◆ **Talyllyn Railway, Tywyn (01654 710472).** Historic steam-operated railway which runs through 7 miles of beautiful countryside, past the scenic Dolgoch Falls, to Abergynolwyn and Nant Gwernol. Railway shop, museum and tearoom.
www.talyllyn.co.uk

Looking for holiday accommodation?
search for details of properties where children are welcome
www.holidayguides.com

☆ Fun for all the Family ☆

SOUTH WALES

Big Pit, Blaenavon (01495 790311). Don a miner's helmet and go down a real coal mine with ex-miners as guides. See the stables where the pit ponies were kept. www.nmgw.ac.uk/bigpit

Cardiff Castle (029 2087 8100). Spanning nearly 2000 years of history, the splendidly decorated apartments are set in a magnificent building surrounded by eight-acre grounds. www.cardiff.gov.uk

The Dinosaur Experience, Great Wedlock (01834 845272). Unique Visitor Centre in 33 acre park, with life-size models, dinosaur trail, hands-on activities; restaurant; picnic areas.

Grove Land, Near Carmarthen (01994 231181). Indoor and outdoor activities for all the family — laser clay pigeon shoot, bumper boats, fun barn, play area, pony rides and lots more.

Heron's Brook Animal Park, Narberth (01834 860723). Set in 30 acres of parkland, where friendly animals roam freely. Feed the rabbits and guinea pigs at Bunny World, enjoy a round of croquet or putting. www.herons-brook.co.uk

Manor House Wild Animal Park, St Florence, Tenby (01646 651201). Pretty grounds with apes, monkeys, otters, deer and an aquarium plus giant slide, radio-controlled boats and other amusements. www.manorhousewildanimalpark.co.uk

Oakwood, Narberth (01834 891373). There's a whole voyage of discovery just waiting to set sail at Oakwood. With more than 40 rides and attractions set in 80 acres of landscaped gardens and parkland, there are absolutely no constraints on fun! www.oakwood-leisure.com

Rhondda Heritage Park, Trehafod (01443 682036). See the story of Black Gold unfold as you tour the site, set in former working colliery. Underground tour, display, visitor centre, tearoom and gift shop. www.rhonddaheritagepark.com

Techniquest, Cardiff (029 2047 5475). Where science and technology come to life - visitors are actively encouraged to handle the exhibits. www.tquest.org.uk

Tredegar House, Newport (01633 815880). "Upstairs, Downstairs" tour, adventure playground, craft workshops, boating lake – something for all the family.

Caldicot Castle & Country Park, Near Chepstow (01291 420241). Explore the castle's fascinating past with an audio tour, and take in the breathtaking views of the 55-acre grounds from the battlements. Children's activity centre, play area. www.caldicotcastle.co.uk

Cantref Adventure Farm, Brecon (01874 665223). Award-winning family attraction with live shows, tractor and trailer rides, new paddle boats and electronic tractors, indoor play area, and Europe's longest sledge ride. www.cantref.com

FREE AND REDUCED RATE HOLIDAY VISITS!
Don't miss our Readers' Offer Vouchers on pages 9-44

See the **Family-Friendly Pubs & Inns**
Supplement on pages 177-180 for establishments
which really welcome children

Ratings & Awards

For the first time ever the AA, VisitBritain, VisitScotland, and the Wales Tourist Board will use a single method of assessing and rating serviced accommodation. Irrespective of which organisation inspects an establishment the rating awarded will be the same, using a common set of standards, giving a clear guide of what to expect. The RAC is no longer operating an Hotel inspection and accreditation business.

Accommodation Standards: Star Grading Scheme

Using a scale of 1-5 stars the objective quality ratings give a clear indication of accommodation standard, cleanliness, ambience, hospitality, service and food, This shows the full range of standards suitable for every budget and preference, and allows visitors to distinguish between the quality of accommodation and facilities on offer in different establishments. All types of board and self-catering accommodation are covered, including hotels, B&Bs, holiday parks, campus accommodation, hostels, caravans and camping, and boats.

VisitBritain and the regional tourist boards, enjoyEngland.com, VisitScotland and VisitWales, and the AA have full details of the grading system on their websites

The more stars, the higher level of quality

★★★★★
exceptional quality, with a degree of luxury

★★★★
excellent standard throughout

★★★
very good level of quality and comfort

★★
good quality, well presented and well run

★
acceptable quality; simple, practical, no frills

National Accessible Scheme

If you have particular mobility, visual or hearing needs, look out for the National Accessible Scheme. You can be confident of finding accommodation or attractions that meet your needs by looking for the following symbols.

 Typically suitable for a person with sufficient mobility to climb a flight of steps but would benefit from fixtures and fittings to aid balance

 Typically suitable for a person with restricted walking ability and for those that may need to use a wheelchair some of the time and can negotiate a maximum of three steps

 Typically suitable for a person who depends on the use of a wheelchair and transfers unaided to and from the wheelchair in a seated position. This person may be an independent traveller

 Typically suitable for a person who depends on the use of a wheelchair in a seated position. This person also requires personal or mechanical assistance (eg carer, hoist).

CLASSIFIED ACCOMMODATION LISTINGS

This is a brief summary of the facilities available at the accommodation featured in this guide. Please note that not all advertisers supply this information, so some entries are not complete - please contact the proprietors directly for full details.

BOARD

🛏 Total number of bedrooms
🛏 Bedrooms with private bath/shower
🍽 Full Board
✕ Bed/Breakfast/ Evening Meal
BB Bed/Breakfast
🍴 Children's meals

SELF-CATERING

🏨 Flats/Apartments
🚐 Caravans
🏠 Chalets/Lodges
🏚 Cottages/Houses
📜 Linen provided
📜 Linen for hire
🧺 On site shop

GENERAL

🍼 Baby listening
🛏 Cots
🪑 Highchairs
📷 Laundry facilities
🐴 Indoor play area
⛰ Outdoor play area
🌐 Children's entertainment
🐕 Pets allowed
♿ Cater for disabled
🍷 Licensed bar
🎵 Live entertainment
☕ Snack bar/food takeaway
🏊 Indoor heated swimming pool
🏊 Outdoor heated swimming pool
◎ Jacuzzi

🌞 Solarium
🎾 Tennis courts
⛳ Putting green
Ⓐ Open all year
🚭 Totally non-smoking

F →2
Child free sharing with parents (eg up to age 2)

R →14
Reductions for children sharing with parents (eg up to age 14)

CORNWALL   Board

CAWSAND • **Wringford Down**
🛏 24 🛏 24   🍼 🛏 🪑 📷 🐴 ⛰   🐕   R   🍷   ▼ on request
✕ BB 🍴   🏊   🎾

MULLION • **Polurrian Hotel**
🛏 39 🛏 39   🍼 🛏 🪑 F→1 🐴 ⛰   R→14   🍷   ▼ on request
✕   🍴   🏊 🏊 ◎ 🌞 🎾 ⛳ Ⓐ

PADSTOW • **Tregea Hotel**
🛏 8   🛏 8   🍷   ▼ on request
       BB   🚭

TRURO • **Trenona Farm**
🛏 4   🛏 4   🛏 🪑   🐕   R   ▼ on request
       BB   🚭

CORNWALL   Self-catering

BROADWOODWIDGER • West Banbury Farm Cottages
▼ on request

FOWEY • Fowey Harbour Cottages
▼ on request

FOWEY • Penquite Farm
▼ on request

HAYLE • St Ives Bay Holiday Park
▼ on request

LAUNCESTON • Bamham Farm Cottages
▼ on request

LAUNCESTON •Forget-Me-Not Farm Holidays
▼ on request

LISKEARD • Cutkive Wood Holiday Lodges
▼ on request

LOOE • Tremaine Green
▼ on request

MARAZION • Trevarthian Holiday Homes
▼ £170

MULLION • Franchis Holidays
▼ on request

NEWQUAY • Trevornick Holiday Park
▼ on request

PADSTOW • Raintree House Holidays
▼ on request

POLPERRO • **Classy Cottages**
▼ on request

PORT GAVERNE• **Green Door Cottages**
▼ on request

TRURO • **Trenona Farm**
▼ on request

SOUTH DEVON   Board

DAWLISH • **Langstone Cliff Hotel**
66   66
▼ on request

EXMOUTH • **Devoncourt Hotel**
▼ on request

KINGSBRIDGE • **Burton Farmhouse**
14   14
▼ on request

TORQUAY • **Red House Hotel**
9   9
▼ on request

SOUTH DEVON   Self-Catering

• **Farm & Cottage Holidays**
▼ on request

• **Toad Hall Cottages**
▼ on request

ASHBURTON • **Parkers Farm Cottages & Caravans**
▼ on request

BRIXHAM • **Devoncourt Holiday Flats**
▼ on request

DAWLISH • **Cofton Country Holidays**
▼ on request

NORTH DEVON   Board

BERRYNARBOR • Sandy Cove Hotel   F → 5   R → 14
🛏 39 🛌 39   ▼ on request

CREDITON • The Oyster
🛏 3 🛌 3   ▼ on request

SOUTH MOLTON • Partridge Arms Farm
🛏 7   ▼ on request

WOOLACOMBE • Woolacombe Bay Hotel
🛏 65 🛌 65   ▼ on request

NORTH DEVON   Self-Catering

ASHWATER • Braddon Cottages & Forest
▼ on request

BARNSTAPLE • North Hill
▼ £210

LITTLE TORRINGTON • Torridge House Farm Cottages
▼ on request

SOUTH MOLTON • West Millbrook
▼ £90

WESTWARD HO! • West Pusehill Farm Cottages
▼ on request

WOOLACOMBE •Woolacombe Bay Holiday Parc
▼ on request

SOMERSET & WILTSHIRE   Board

SALISBURY • Hayburn Wyke   R → 14
▼ £26.00

STOGUMBER • **Wick House**
5 5 ▼ on request

WESTBURY • **Spinney Farmhouse**
3 ▼ on request

WESTON-SUPER-MARE • **Batch Country Hotel** [R]
11 11 ▼ on request

WHEDDON CROSS • **Exmoor House**
5 5 ▼ on request

SOMERSET & WILTSHIRE   Self-Catering

CHEDDAR • **Sungate Holiday Apartments**
▼ on request

TAUNTON • **Quantock Orchard Caravan Park**
▼ on request

HAMPSHIRE & DORSET   Board

BARTON-ON-SEA • **Laurel Lodge**
3 3 ▼ £25.00

BOURNEMOUTH • **Denewood Hotel**
12 ▼ on request

LULWORTH COVE • **Cromwell House** [F] → 2   [R] → 13
17 17 ▼ on request

RINGWOOD • **High Corner Inn**
7 7 ▼ on request

STUDLAND BAY • **Knoll House** [R] → 12
80 56 ▼ on request

HAMPSHIRE & DORSET   Self-Catering

BEAMINSTER • Orchand End/Old Coach House

▼ £300

BRIDPORT • Lancombes House

Ⓐ   ▼ on request

CHARMOUTH • Cardsmill Farm Holidays

▼ on request

ISLE OF WIGHT   Board

SANDOWN • Fernside Hotel
11   11

▼ on request

SANDOWN • Sandhill Hotel

▼ £37.00

SANDOWN • St Catherine's Hotel
19   19

Ⓐ   ▼ on request

TOTLAND • Frenchman's Cove
10   10

▼ on request

ISLE OF WIGHT   Self-Catering

• Island Cottage Holidays

▼ £185
Ⓐ   ▲ £1595

RYDE • Hillgrove Park

▼ on request

YARMOUTH • The Orchards Holiday Park

Ⓐ   ▼ on request

FHG Guides
**publish a large range of well-known accommodation guides.
We will be happy to send you details or you can use
the order form at the back of this book.**

SUSSEX — Board

CHICHESTER • Woodstock House Hotel
🛏 13   🛁 13   BB   (A)   ▼ on request

HAILSHAM • Longleys Farm Cottage   R
🛏 3   🛁 2   BB   ▼ £21.00

LEWES • Tamberry Hall
🛏 3   🛁 3   BB   ▼ on request

SUSSEX — Self-Catering

CHIDDINGLY • Pekes
▼ on request

SELSEY • Bunn Leisure
▼ on request

KENT — Board

ASHFORD • Bolden's Wood
🛏 3   BB   ▼ £25.00

CANTERBURY • Great Field Farm   R
🛏 3   🛁 3   BB   ▼ £30.00

DOVER • Maison Dieu Guest House
🛏 7   🛁 5   BB   (A)   ▼ on request

HEADCORN • Waterkant Guest House
🛏 3   BB   (A)   ▼ £20.00

LONDON & HOME COUNTIES — Board

KINGSTON-UPON-THAMES • Chase Lodge
🛏 11   🛁 11   BB   (A)   ▼ on request

LONDON • Gower Hotel
🛏 21   🛁 19   BB   (A)   ▼ on request

LONDON • Athena Hotel

BB   Ⓐ   ▼ on request

LONDON • Queens Hotel

BB   Ⓐ   ▼ on request

LONDON • Barry House Hotel

🛏 18   🛁 15
BB   ▼ on request

LONDON • The Darlington

🛏 40   🛁 40
BB   Ⓐ   🚭   ▼ on request

EAST ANGLIA   Board

FRAMLINGHAM • High House Farm

🛏 2   🛁 2   🛏 🚼   🎢   ▼ on request
BB

EAST ANGLIA   Self-Catering

BACTON-ON-SEA • Castaways Holiday Park

🏠   🏕   📺   🎢   🐴   🍷   ▼ on request
🧺   🎵 ☕   Ⓐ

FOXLEY • Moor Farm Stable Cottages

🏡   🐴   ▼ on request
   🦢

HENLEY • Damerons Farm Holidays

🏡   🛏 🚼   🎢   🐴   ▼ on request
🗂   Ⓐ

KESSINGLAND • Kessingland Cottage

🏡   🐴 ♿   ▼ £95
    ▲ £375

MIDLANDS   Board

ASHBOURNE • Dog & Partridge Inn

🛏 30   🛁 28   🛁 🛏 🚼   🐎 🎢   🐴   🍷   ▼ on request
❌ BB 🍽   Ⓐ

BUXTON • Alison Park Hotel

🛏 17   🛁 17   🐴 ♿ 🍷   ▼ on request
🍴 ❌ BB 🍽

GREAT MALVERN • Croft Guest House
🛏 5 🛏 3 ✗ BB · · · 🐕 · 🍷 🚭 · ▼ on request

HENLEY-ON-THAMES • The Old Bakery
🛏 3 BB · · · Ⓐ · ▼ on request

MALVERN WELLS • Brickbarns Farm
🛏 3 🍼 🛏 BB · · · ▼ £20.00

TELFORD • Holiday Inn
🛏 150 🛏 150 🛏 🪑 ✗ BB 🍴 ☕ · ◎ · Ⓐ · 🍷 · ▼ on request

TELFORD • International Hotel
🛏 101 🛏 101 🛏 🪑 ✗ BB 🍴 ☕ · Ⓐ · 🍷 · ▼ on request

MIDLANDS · Self-Catering

LUDLOW • Sutton Court Farm
🏠 · 🐕 · 🚭 · ▼ on request

STANTON BY BRIDGE • Woodland Hills Court Cottages
🏠 · ▼ on request

WATERHOUSES • Field Head Farmhouse Holidays
🏠 🛏 🛝 🐕 · ◎ · Ⓐ 🚭 · ▼ on request

NORTH-EAST ENGLAND · Board

BAMBURGH • Mizen Head Hotel
🛏 ✗ BB · · · 🐕 · 🍷 · Ⓐ · ▼ on request

YORK • Blossoms
🛏 15 BB · · · 🍷 · Ⓐ · ▼ on request

NORTH-EAST ENGLAND · Self-Catering

BISHOP AUCKLAND • Low Lands Farm Cottages
🏠 🍼 🛏 🪑 🛝 🐕 · ▼ £160 ▲ £340

WHITBY • Greenhouses Farm Cottages
🏠 🛝 · ▼ £225 ▲ £600

NORTH-WEST ENGLAND   Board

AMBLESIDE • **Rothay Manor**   F → 3   R → 16
🛏 19   🛏 19   ⬤ 🏛 👤   ♿ ♀ ▼ on request
✕ BB 🍴   ⊘

CONISTON • **Waterhead Hotel**
🛏 22   🛏 22   🏛   🐕 ♿ ♀ ▼ on request
✕ BB   ⊘

LYTHAM ST ANNES • **Chadwick Hotel**   F → 2   R → 12
🛏 75   🛏 75   ⬤ 🏛 👤 📺 🎠   ♀ ▼ on request
🍽 ✕ BB 🍴   ♫ ☕ 🎣   ◉ 🏠   Ⓐ

ST ANNES • **Dalmeny Hotel**   R → 16
🛏 128   🛏 128   ⬤ 🏛 👤 📺 🎠   ✇   ♀ ▼ on request
✕ BB 🍴   ♫ ☕ 🎣   ◉ 🏠

WINDERMERE • **Green Gables**
🛏 7   🛏 7   ♀ ▼ £23.00
BB   Ⓐ

NORTH-WEST ENGLAND   Self-Catering

AMBLESIDE • **Greenhowe Caravan Park**
🚐   🏛 📺   🐕 ▼ on request
🗄 🧺

SCOTLAND   Board

BALLACHULISH • Loch Leven Hotel
🛏 12   🛆 12   🐕   🍷   ▼ £40.00
🍴 BB 🪑 ♫

CATACOL • Catacol Bay Hotel   F → 3   R → 12
🛏 6   🐕   🍷   ▼ on request
🍴 BB 🪑 ♫   Ⓐ

DALMALLY • Rockhill Waterside Country House
🛏 5   🐕   ▼ on request
BB ♫

WHITHORN • Craiglemine Cottage   F → 6   R → 16
🛏 2   🐕   ▼ £23.00
🍴 BB   🚭

SCOTLAND   Self-Catering

AVIEMORE • Cairngorm Highland Bungalows
🏡   🐕   ▼ on request
Ⓐ

AVIEMORE • Speyside Leisure Park
🚐 🏠   ⛰   ♿   ▼ on request
📑   🏃

DALBEATTIE • Barend Holiday Village
🏠   📻   ⛰   🍷   ▼ on request
📑   🏃

OBAN • Melfort Pier & Harbour
🏡   🏛 🧗   🐕 ♿   ▼ £90.00
☕

OBAN • Cologin
🏠 🏡   📻   🐕 ♿ 🍷   ▼ on request
📑 📰 🧺   🚭

TARBERT • Barfad Farmlands
🏡   🏛 📻   ▼ on request
📑

THORNHILL • Hope Cottage
🏡   🐕   ▼ on request
📑

WALES — Board

ABERDOVEY • Trefeddian Hotel ▫→ 16 ▼ £54.00
🛏 59 🍴 59

ABERPORTH • Highcliffe Hotel ▼ on request
🛏 15 🍴 14

DOLGELLAU • Tyn-y-Groes Hotel ▫F→ 2 ▫R→ 9 ▼ on request

LLANGOLLEN • Wynnstay Arms ▼ on request
🛏 7 🍴 7

WALES — Self-catering

CONWY VALLEY • Trefriw Cottages ▼ on request

GOODWICK • Carne Farm ▼ on request

HAVERFORDWEST • Scamford Caravan Park ▼ on request

LLANTEG • Llanteglos Estate ▼ on request

WELSHPOOL • Madog's Wells ▼ £150.00t

See the Family-Friendly Pubs & Inns
Supplement on pages 177-180 for establishments
which really welcome children

Family-Friendly Pubs and Inns

This is a selection of establishments which make an extra effort to cater for parents and children. The majority provide a separate children's menu or they may be willing to serve small portions of main course dishes on request; there are often separate outdoor or indoor play areas where the junior members of the family can let off steam while Mum and Dad unwind over a drink.

For details of more properties which welcome children, see the FHG website
www.holidayguides.com

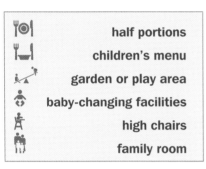

half portions

children's menu

garden or play area

baby-changing facilities

high chairs

family room

THE BELL HOTEL
Market Square, Winslow,
Buckinghamshire MK18 3AB
Tel: 01296 714091
www.thebell-hotel.com

VICTORIA INN
Perranuthnoe, Near Penzance,
Cornwall TR20 9NP
Tel: 01736 710309
www.victoriainn-penzance.co.uk

CROOKED INN
Stoketon Cross, Trematon,
Saltash, Cornwall PL12 4RZ
Tel: 01752 848177
www.crooked-inn.co.uk

TOWER BANK ARMS
Near Sawrey, Ambleside,
Cumbria LA22 0LF
Tel: 015394 36334
www.towerbankarms.com

BROOK HOUSE INN
Boot, Eskdale,
Cumbria CA19 1TG
Tel: 019467 23288
www.brookhouseinn.co.uk

KING GEORGE IV
Eskdale Green, Holmrook,
Cumbria CA19 1TS
Tel: 01946 723262
www.kinggeorge-eskdale.co.uk

GILPIN BRIDGE
Bridge End, Levens,
Near Kendal, Cumbria LA8 8EP
Tel: 015395 52206
www.gilpinbridgeinn.co.uk

GREYHOUND HOTEL
Main Street, Shap, Penrith,
Cumbria CA10 3PW
Tel: 01931 716474
www.greyhoundshap.co.uk

DALESMAN INN
Main Street, Sedbergh,
Cumbria LA10 5BN
Tel: 015396 21183
www.thedalesman.co.uk

DOLPHIN INN
Kingston, Near Kingsbridge,
Devon TQ7 4QE
Tel: 01548 810314
www.dolphin-inn.co.uk

MALTSTERS ARMS
Bow Creek, Tuckenhay,
Near Totnes, Devon TQ9 7EQ
Tel: 01803 732350
www.tuckenhay.com

THE CRICKETERS
Clavering, Near Saffron Walden,
Essex CB11 4QT
Tel: 01799 550442
www.thecricketers.co.uk

KING'S HEAD INN
Birdwood, Near Huntley,
Gloucestershire GL19 3EF
Tel: 01452 750348
www.kingsheadbirdwood.co.uk

RHYDSPENCE INN

Whitney-on-Wye, Near Hay-on-Wye,
Herefordshire HR3 6EU
Tel: 01497 831262
www.rhydspence-inn.co.uk

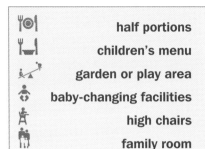

half portions

children's menu

garden or play area

baby-changing facilities

high chairs

family room

SARACENS HEAD INN

Symonds Yat East, Ross-on-Wye,
Herefordshire HR9 6JL
Tel: 01600 890435
www.saracensheadinn.co.uk

CHEQUERS INN

The Street, Smarden,
Near Ashford, Kent TN27 8QA
Tel: 01233 770217
www.thechequerssmarden.com

WHITE HORSE INN

The Street, Boughton,
Kent ME13 9AX
Tel: 01227 751343
www.whitehorsecanterbury.co.uk

WHIPPER-IN HOTEL

Market Place, Oakham,
Leicestershire & Rutland LE15 6DT
Tel: 01572 756971
www.brook-hotels.co.uk

COOK AND BARKER

Newtown-on-the-Moor, Morpeth,
Northumberland NE65 9JY
Tel: 01665 575234
www.cookandbarkerinn.co.uk

TOLLGATE INN

Church Street, Kingham,
Oxfordshire OX7 6YA
Tel: 01608 658389
www.thetollgate.com

THE FLOWER POT
Ferry Lane, Henley-on-Thames,
Oxfordshire RG9 3DG
Tel: 01491 574721

MYTTON AND MERMAID
Atcham, Shrewsbury,
Shropshire SY5 6QG
Tel: 01743 761220
www.myttonandmermaid.co.uk

THE LAMB INN
High Street, Hindon
Wiltshire SP3 6DP
Tel: 01747 820573
www.lambathindon.co.uk

FAIRFAX ARMS
Gilling East, York,
North Yorkshire YO62 4JH
Tel: 01439 788212
www.fairfaxarms.co.uk

CARISBROOKE
Drumduan Road, Forres,
Aberdeen, Banff & Moray IV36 1BS
Tel: 01309 672585
www.carisbrooke-hotel.co.uk

ABERDOUR HOTEL
38 High Street, Aberdour,
Fife KY3 0SW
Tel: 01383 860325
www.aberdourhotel.co.uk

WELL COUNTRY INN
Main Street, Scotlandwell, Kinross,
Perth & Kinross KY13 9JA
Tel: 01592 840444
www.thewellcountryinn.co.uk

CASTLE VIEW HOTEL
16 Bridge Street, Chepstow,
Monmouthshire NP16 5EZ
Tel: 01291 620349
www.hotelchepstow.co.uk

Index of towns and sections
Please also refer to Contents page 3

Ratings & Awards

For the first time ever the AA, VisitBritain, VisitScotland, and the Wales Tourist Board will use a single method of assessing and rating serviced accommodation. Irrespective of which organisation inspects an establishment the rating awarded will be the same, using a common set of standards, giving a clear guide of what to expect. The RAC is no longer operating an Hotel inspection and accreditation business.

Accommodation Standards: Star Grading Scheme

Using a scale of 1-5 stars the objective quality ratings give a clear indication of accommodation standard, cleanliness, ambience, hospitality, service and food, This shows the full range of standards suitable for every budget and preference, and allows visitors to distinguish between the quality of accommodation and facilities on offer in different establishments. All types of board and self-catering accommodation are covered, including hotels, B&Bs, holiday parks, campus accommodation, hostels, caravans and camping, and boats.

VisitBritain and the regional tourist boards, enjoyEngland.com, VisitScotland and VisitWales, and the AA have full details of the grading system on their websites

The more stars, the higher level of quality

★★★★★
exceptional quality, with a degree of luxury

★★★★
excellent standard throughout

★★★
very good level of quality and comfort

★★
good quality, well presented and well run

★
acceptable quality; simple, practical, no frills

National Accessible Scheme

If you have particular mobility, visual or hearing needs, look out for the National Accessible Scheme. You can be confident of finding accommodation or attractions that meet your needs by looking for the following symbols.

 Typically suitable for a person with sufficient mobility to climb a flight of steps but would benefit from fixtures and fittings to aid balance

 Typically suitable for a person with restricted walking ability and for those that may need to use a wheelchair some of the time and can negotiate a maximum of three steps

 Typically suitable for a person who depends on the use of a wheelchair and transfers unaided to and from the wheelchair in a seated position. This person may be an independent traveller

 Typically suitable for a person who depends on the use of a wheelchair in a seated position. This person also requires personal or mechanical assistance (eg carer, hoist).

Other FHG titles for 2008

FHG Guides Ltd have a large range of attractive holiday accommodation guides for all kinds of holiday opportunities throughout Britain. They also make useful gifts at any time of year.
Our guides are available in most bookshops and larger newsagents but we will be happy to post you a copy direct if you have any difficulty. POST FREE for addresses in the UK. We will also post abroad but have to charge separately for post or freight.

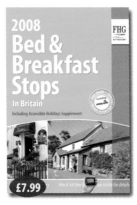

The original Farm Holiday Guide to COAST & COUNTRY HOLIDAYS in England, Scotland, Wales and Channel Islands. Board, Self-catering, Caravans/Camping, Activity Holidays.

BED AND BREAKFAST STOPS Over 1000 friendly and comfortable overnight stops. Non-smoking, Disabled and Special Diets Supplements.

BRITAIN'S BEST LEISURE & RELAXATION GUIDE A quick-reference general guide for all kinds of holidays.

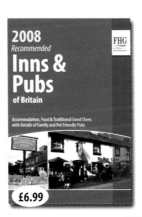

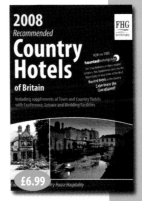

The Original PETS WELCOME! The bestselling guide to holidays for pet owners and their pets.

Recommended INNS & PUBS of Britain Including Pubs, Inns and Small Hotels,

Recommended COUNTRY HOTELS of Britain Including Country Houses, for the discriminating.

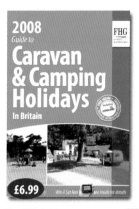

SELF-CATERING HOLIDAYS in Britain ☐
Over 1000 addresses throughout for self-catering and caravans in Britain.

The FHG Guide to CARAVAN & CAMPING HOLIDAYS ☐
Caravans for hire, sites and holiday parks and centres.

Recommended SHORT BREAK HOLIDAYS IN BRITAIN & IRELAND ☐
"Approved" accommodation for quality bargain breaks.

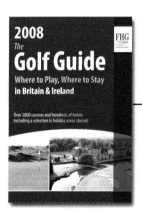

The GOLF GUIDE – *Where to play Where to stay*
In association with GOLF MONTHLY. Over 2800 golf courses in Britain with convenient accommodation. Holiday Golf in France, Portugal, Spain, USA and Thailand.

 £9.99 ☐

Tick your choice above and send your order and payment to

**FHG Guides Ltd. Abbey Mill Business Centre
Seedhill, Paisley, Scotland PA1 1TJ
TEL: 0141- 887 0428 • FAX: 0141- 889 7204
e-mail: admin@fhguides.co.uk**

FHG

Deduct 10% for 2/3 titles or copies; 20% for 4 or more.

Send to: NAME ....

ADDRESS ....

....

....

POST CODE ....

I enclose Cheque/Postal Order for £ ....

SIGNATURE ....DATE ....

Please complete the following to help us improve the service we provide.
How did you find out about our guides?:

☐ Press   ☐ Magazines   ☐ TV/Radio   ☐ Family/Friend   ☐ Other